DONEGAL TABLE

BRIAN McDERMOTT is an award-winning chef who is passionate about sharing his love of food with others. As a host, presenter and demonstrator, he is one of the most sought-after chefs on the Irish food-festival circuit. He also runs his own cookery school in Moville, County Donegal and is a food consultant to some of the best-known names in Irish food. He is the author of the successful cookery book *Reunite with Food* and is a regular on RTÉ and BBC television and radio, and in the local and national press. He lives in Moville with his wife, Brenda, and daughters, Niamh and Aoife.

BRIAN McDERMOTT'S

DONEGAL TABLE

DELICIOUS EVERYDAY COOKING

THE O'BRIEN PRESS
DUBLIN

First published 2018 by
The O'Brien Press Ltd,
12 Terenure Road East, Rathgar, Dublin 6, D06 HD27, Ireland.
Tel: +353 1 4923333; Fax: +353 1 4922777
E-mail: books@obrien.ie; Website: www.obrien.ie
The O'Brien Press is a member of Publishing Ireland.

ISBN: 978-1-84717-979-1

Photography by A Fox in the Kitchen.
Lough Swilly from Grianán Of Aileach, County Donegal, Ireland by Michelle Holihan (cover)
courtesy of Shutterstock.
Brian McDermott with Neven Maguire, page 13, courtesy of Lorraine Teevan Photography.
Photographs on pages 100–101, 118–119, 130–131 and 152–153 courtesy of Carsten Krieger.

6 5 4 3 2 1
21 20 19 18

Printed by EDELVIVES, Spain
The paper in this book is produced using pulp from managed forests

Published in

DUBLIN
UNESCO
City of Literature

ACKNOWLEDGEMENTS

I've been a chef for almost twenty-five years now, and it's been an amazing journey. There are so many people I want to thank for their love, help and support along the way. Firstly, my parents, Brian and Mary, who have been my foundation since long before I even thought of becoming a chef. My wife, Brenda, who is the constant light in my life, and our two daughters, Niamh and Aoife, who have both made a huge contribution to this book. I'm so proud of them and everything they do. My brothers and sisters and their families, Brenda's parents, Seamus and Veronica, and Brenda's siblings and their families have all been such a positive part of my life and career.

My neighbours, who supply the wonderful produce I cook with every day, and in particular the fishermen of Greencastle Harbour and the Norris family of potato and beef farmers who not only provided me with the ingredients for many of these recipes but willingly posed for photographs as well!

Neven Maguire has been an inspiration, a mentor and a great friend to me from the earliest days of my career. His family and his team have also been so supportive of me, in particular Kenny, Gerry, Andrea and Claire.

My agent, Freya McClements, project-managed this book from the idea stage right through to the launch, and her experience and advice have been priceless. Thanks to everyone at The O'Brien Press – especially Michael O'Brien, Ivan O'Brien, Emma Byrne, Aoife Walsh and Emma Dunne. The dedication, commitment and encouragement from the whole team has been beyond my expectation. Thanks also to Zeta and Rob from A Fox in the Kitchen for their wonderful photography, and Claire Beasley who proofread this book.

Thanks to my own team – Eileen Mc Laughlin, Breda Harkin, Aileen Duffy and John and Marie Duffy. Also to Seamus, Sean and the team at Inishowen Motors for keeping me on the road in style over the past few years.

A massive thank you to BBC Radio Foyle and the *Mark Patterson Show* for allowing me to talk and cook food for their listeners every Wednesday. Thanks also to RTÉ's *Today Show* and all the team in Cork, in particular, Daithí Ó Sé, Maura Derrane, Colm Crowley and Rory Corby.

I also want to thank the numerous food festivals that invite me to cook and MC across Ireland each year, especially Bord Bia, Hylda Adams and all the team at Bloom. I am also proud to have the support of my superb brand partners, the National Dairy Council, Clarke's Fresh Fruit and McElhinney's of Ballybofey – a sincere thanks for your continued support. Thank you also to my colleagues in the Foodovation Centre at the North West Regional College in Derry.

And finally, to the many others who are too numerous to mention but to whom I owe a debt of gratitude, thank you. You have all made these recipes possible, and for that I am truly grateful.

Contents

Foreword

I've been lucky enough to be a friend of Brian's for more than twenty years, so I was honoured when he asked me to write the foreword for this book. If I'm honest, I'll admit I've been hassling him for years about another cookery book, and I know he was probably fed up with me asking him when he was going to write down all his wonderful Donegal recipes! Now that it's here, I couldn't be more proud of the finished product – and I know he couldn't be happier with it. Brian's a Donegal man through and through – it's the coolest place on the planet, he keeps reminding me! – and he's spent his career championing his county's great local produce and making great home cooking accessible. This is the book I've been waiting for from Brian.

We first met in Donegal – where else? I was doing a cookery demo up in Killybegs and Brian was there doing his degree. We got chatting and just clicked – and really it was as simple as that. I think it's fair to say I warmed to him immediately. He was always someone I'd admired and respected as a chef, but from then on, we seemed to keep meeting at lots of different food events, and the more I met him, the more he stood out. Partly it's his personality – everyone who knows Brian will tell you he's a gentleman and a really nice guy, and he's someone I have great craic with. We have huge respect for each other but we also have huge fun, and I think there's something about our personalities that means we just bounce off each other really well. One of the best things about having chef friends is that we all share the same passion for food – truthfully, we're all a little bit obsessed with it – but Brian's love and enthusiasm for what he does is infectious. If you've seen him in action at cookery demos, you'll agree – it's why I always say he's the most versatile chef in Ireland. Whether he's demonstrating his cooking at food festivals or keeping us all in order as MC, he has a unique ability to connect with people and to share his recipes with them in an achievable way, and that shone through when I read this book. That's just the kind of chef he is. I know this is one of those books that will sit on kitchen counters and end up covered in flour and goodness knows what else because you'll find yourself using it again and again.

One of the things Brian and I have in common is that we both come from big families, and the food our mams cooked at home was where our love of food began for both of us. Inishowen, where he's from, has some incredible food producers, and of course he has fabulous seafood right on his doorstep at Greencastle. At home in Blacklion we get all our fish for the restaurant from Donegal, and my favourite of Brian's recipes would have to be his Wild Atlantic Way Fish Pie. There's something very comforting as well as nourishing about it, and with homemade wheaten bread it's hard to beat.

In recent years, I think people in Ireland have become more and more particular about where their food comes from, and I know many people who now make a point of buying seasonal Irish produce from the family butcher or the local fishmonger. Ireland has always had great food, and while we may have been known for those traditional dishes, our bacon and cabbage, our stew, our soda bread, now we're lucky enough to have a new generation of Irish chefs like Brian who are showcasing it in their cooking. There's a story behind every dish, and one of the things I love about Brian is that he can tell you exactly where all his ingredients come from. It was only when I travelled around Donegal with him, meeting food producers and seeing some of the fabulous locations, like Grianán an Aileach and its award-winning local beef, that I realised just how unique a county it is. Yet, somehow, he's managed to sum it all up in this beautiful book, which is full of the tradition, expertise and local knowledge that he loves to share with his audiences, his friends and family, and his readers. I can't think of a better way to connect with food and with cooking, and when I read Brian's book I'm inspired by the thought of trying and sharing some of these recipes. It really is an exciting time to be a chef in Ireland. I consider myself privileged to be a part of it – and I feel even more privileged that Brian is too.

Neven Maguire
Proprietor, MacNean House & Restaurant

Introduction

As one of twelve children growing up in Bridgend and the parish of Burt on the Inishowen Peninsula in County Donegal, my mother's kitchen table was the focal point of the family. She was always there, cooking and baking, usually with one or two of us at her feet trying to scran a slice of soda bread or a piece of cake. When all twelve of us were around it could get pretty crowded, but even from a young age I loved the sense of belonging I felt in that kitchen – me and my parents and my brothers and sisters, all sitting down to eat together. I loved the craic, too – many's the story that was told around that table, especially when relatives or neighbours called in!

I didn't realise it at the time, of course, but it was some achievement keeping us all fed and happy in the days before microwaves, ready-meals and takeaways. We ate what my father would have called 'good, honest food'. There was always a pot of stew on the go and plenty of spuds. It was only later that I realised that practically everything we ate was local. Our meat and vegetables came from local farms, and our fish came straight from the pier at Greencastle and could be in the pan within the hour. My dad could have told you the field our dinner came from or the fisherman who had caught it.

Looking back, I realise that my own journey with food started at that kitchen table. My mother will tell you I always loved to eat, but I always loved to cook too. Even from a young age, food for me was something to be shared, and I think that's what inspired me to become a chef – that desire to create food which would give others that same sense of belonging I felt at my mother's kitchen table. She even got me my first job in the food business, as a kitchen porter in Harry's Restaurant in Bridgend, when I was fifteen. Mum was already working there, and for a year we worked side by side and I learnt everything I ever wanted to know about scrubbing pots and pans! But I found I loved being around the busy environment of the restaurant – and a year later I started to learn my trade in the main kitchen.

I've always described that period of my life, when I was working in busy kitchens in hotels and restaurants, as a rollercoaster – I loved the hectic, adrenaline-filled world of catering and the buzz it gave me. At the age of thirty-three, my life came crashing down around me when I was diagnosed with a life-threatening heart condition. I was warned that if I kept working in the hot, high-stress kitchen environment, I would have another heart attack – and I might not survive. Ironically, it turned out to be the biggest opportunity of my life. I was forced to re-evaluate my lifestyle, my diet – everything. And it led me back to my mother's table.

As I recovered from my illness, I began to teach cookery skills to community groups, and I realised there was, quite literally, an appetite out there for Donegal food. I believe that tasty, healthy food based around traditional Donegal recipes and local produce is something everyone can make and enjoy – and these days I'm lucky enough to be able to share that message at food festivals, on television and radio, in my own cookery school and as a consultant to the Irish food industry.

Of course, I also have my own Donegal table to cook for. My wife, Brenda, and I have always tried to bring up our two daughters, Niamh and Aoife, with the same values we were reared with, and making time to sit down and eat as a family is a huge part of that. These are our recipes – and, for me, they sum up the best of what Donegal has to offer for your table. It's what inspires me every day – and I hope it will inspire you too.

Brian

My Store Cupboard

There are some ingredients I always have on hand in my kitchen presses. They're my essentials for making tasty home-cooked meals every time – and if you can buy local, so much the better!

MY TOP TEN STORE-CUPBOARD INGREDIENTS

1. Vinegars – balsamic, white wine and apple cider
2. Rice
3. Selection of pastas
4. Barley
5. Tinned tomatoes
6. Selection of spices – especially nutmeg, cinnamon, cumin, chilli and turmeric
7. Worcestershire sauce
8. Mustard
9. Honey
10. Rapeseed oil

And my final must-have?
Seriously good coffee!

My Kitchen Garden

It's no exaggeration to say my kitchen garden is a vital part of my cooking. I love fresh herbs so I put in a lot of effort to make sure I have some available all year round. My garden is just outside my cookery school, so fresh produce is literally only metres away when I'm cooking!

I wasn't a natural gardener – I started out a few years ago with just some chives and rosemary and have gradually added more. Now I even grow fruit and vegetables – they're simply so much tastier than the shop-bought variety.

Having fresh herbs on hand doesn't have to be time consuming – just a few pots on a windowsill can provide a great supply of sage or thyme, which will add depth and flavour to your dishes.

I think what I love most about fresh herbs is that they constantly challenge me to experiment and try new things when I'm cooking, and I promise you'll love experimenting too!

MY TOP FIVE HERBS

1. Thyme
2. Rosemary
3. Sage
4. Parsley
5. Basil

GETTING TO KNOW DONEGAL

As a chef, I often think how lucky I am to come from Donegal.
We get more rainfall than anywhere else in Ireland, so our pastures are
greener, and it really does make our produce extra special. My neighbours are potato farmers, dairy farmers, bakers and fishermen – and
I love nothing better than heading out first thing in the morning to
see what they have for me. These recipes are all inspired by my many
mornings out and about meeting food producers and are ideal for a
picnic lunch or snack.

Crispy Summer Mackerel on Toast

Mackerel literally jump out of Lough Foyle in the summer months. It's the nearest most of us will ever come to free food, and you'll see plenty of dads and kids on the pier in Moville catching dinner! For me, the lime juice and rocket pesto really bring out that summery feel.

SERVES 4

For the pesto

Good handful of rocket

3 tbsp rapeseed oil

2 cloves of garlic

2 tbsp red wine vinegar

Freshly ground black pepper

50 g blue cheese (or cheese of your choice)

4 tsp sesame seeds

For the mackerel

1 tsp chilli powder

Freshly ground black pepper

50 g plain flour

4 slices ciabatta bread

200 ml rapeseed oil

4 mackerel fillets

60 g crème fraiche

1 lime, cut into 4 wedges

1. To make the pesto, put all the ingredients except the sesame seeds in a blender and combine until you have a smooth-ish paste. Toast the sesame seeds on a flat, dry pan until golden brown, making sure you stay at the pan and toss them continuously. Add them to the blended pesto.

2. For the mackerel, first combine the chilli powder and black pepper with the flour.

3. Toast the slices of ciabatta bread and drizzle with some of the rapeseed oil, then set aside.

4. Heat a wok and add the rest of the rapeseed oil. Pat both sides of the mackerel fillets in the flour then place in the hot oil. Cook each fillet for about 2 minutes on each side, until crispy.

5. Spoon some crème fraiche onto each slice of ciabatta and place a piece of mackerel on top. Drizzle with rocket pesto and a squeeze of lime.

BRIAN'S TIP

Pesto will keep for three weeks in a sealed container in the fridge. It tastes great with pork, chicken, salads and pasta.

Surf 'n' Turf Sliders

Sliders are a great way to welcome guests to your home. This combination gives a great taste of the sea and the land that produce the great seafood and beef we are famous for in Donegal.

SERVES 4

For the burgers

1 small onion, diced

Drizzle of rapeseed oil

400 g minced beef

1 egg

Pinch of nutmeg

30 g breadcrumbs

50 g Cheddar cheese, grated

For the dressing

75 g mayonnaise

4 gherkins

12 capers

Squeeze of lemon juice

To serve

100 g Malin Head crab meat

8 mini brioche buns

8 slices of tomato

1. Preheat the oven to 180°C/350°F/Gas Mark 4.
2. For the burgers, fry the diced onion in the oil. Place the minced beef in a bowl, then add the cooked onion, egg, nutmeg and breadcrumbs. Add the grated cheese and combine to form eight evenly shaped mini burgers. Set aside.
3. To make the tartare dressing, put all the ingredients in a blender and blitz.
4. Mix the dressing with the crab meat.
5. Fry the mini burgers in a pan for 3 minutes on each side, then transfer to the oven to cook through in the centre.
6. Toast the brioche buns.
7. To serve, place a mini burger on each brioche-bun base. Add a slice of tomato and a spoonful of the crab-meat mix and then put the other half of the bun on top.

BRIAN'S TIP

Replace the crab with freshly grilled prawns.

Bacon on Eggy Bread with Field Mushrooms

Eggy bread is one of life's pleasures when done right. Top it with crispy bacon and mushrooms and it's perfect for any occasion. We like to use batch loaf in our house, cut thick and always fresh.

SERVES 4

8 rashers dry-cured streaky bacon

4 eggs

50 ml milk

Pinch of cinnamon

Freshly ground black pepper

4 slices of bread (preferably batch loaf, see page 128)

Drizzle of rapeseed oil

50 g butter

8 mushrooms, sliced

Sprig of fresh thyme

Handful of rocket leaves

40 g tomato ketchup

1. Heat the grill and grill the bacon until crispy.
2. Whisk the eggs in a bowl with the milk, cinnamon and a twist of black pepper.
3. Place the bread in the egg mix for one minute to soak.
4. Heat a large frying pan and add a drizzle of oil and half of the butter. Add the slices of bread and cook on medium heat until golden brown on both sides.
5. Place the bread in a warm oven, and in the same pan add the rest of the butter and fry the sliced mushrooms with the sprig of thyme and some more black pepper.
6. Serve the bread with the rocket, bacon, mushrooms and a dollop of ketchup.

BRIAN'S TIP

This is also great with quality sausages from your local butcher.

My Ultimate Open Farm Sandwich

Any sandwich is made instantly better with a homemade ploughman's pickle. My pickle recipe is easy to make and keeps for months in the fridge. Leftover cooked beef from a Sunday roast is perfect for this sandwich.

SERVES 4

For the ploughman's pickle

1 onion, diced

1 courgette, diced

150 g carrots, peeled and diced

150 g turnip, peeled and diced

4 cloves of garlic, crushed

1 cucumber, diced

Juice of 1 lemon

200 ml malt vinegar

175 g brown sugar

1 tbsp ground allspice

For the sandwich

1 onion, sliced

Drizzle of rapeseed oil

Freshly ground black pepper

4 slices of ciabatta

1 iceberg lettuce

400 g cooked leftover beef

8 slices of tomato

4 slices of mature Cheddar

1. To make the pickle, place all the ingredients in a pot and simmer until the turnips are cooked and the pickle is almost sticky. If the consistency becomes too thick, add a drop of boiling water to loosen it. When cooked and cooled, place in sterilised jars with a lid and seal.

2. For the sandwich, first fry the onion in the oil and season with pepper.

3. Heat the bread in the oven or under the grill. Place a few leaves of lettuce on each piece of warm bread and arrange thin slices of the leftover beef on top. Next, arrange the tomato slices and spread with the warm onions and then the slices of cheese.

4. Top with the pickle.

BRIAN'S TIP

Add a layer of mustard or mayonnaise to the warm bread for added flavour.

BBQ Prawns on the Beach

Summer in Donegal means a barbecue on the beach. A disposable barbecue is perfect for prawns, as they cook so quickly, and you can make the tasty butter at home to drizzle on them as they are cooking. Sun, sea and prawns equals heaven to me.

SERVES 4

For the butter

1 small red chilli

1 clove of garlic, crushed

Zest of 1 lemon

Freshly ground black pepper

150 g butter, softened

For the prawns

1 kg whole prawns

1 lemon, cut into 4 wedges

Handful of fresh chopped parsley

1. To make the butter, finely chop the chilli and mix with the crushed garlic, lemon zest and pepper. Add in softened butter and mix well.

2. Place a sheet of greaseproof paper on the counter and roll the butter inside it to form a cylinder shape, like a thick sausage. Place in the cooler box you are taking to the beach.

3. Light the barbecue and allow the charcoal to turn grey. Split the prawns in half lengthways and place on the barbecue. Cook for 4 minutes on each side.

4. Move the prawns to the outer edge of the barbecue. Thinly slice the butter and allow it to melt on top of the prawns. Serve with a squeeze of lemon juice and a sprinkle of freshly chopped parsley.

BRIAN'S TIP

Always barbecue on charcoal for an authentic flavour.

GROWN HERE, NOT FLOWN HERE

I always try to use locally grown produce, rather than out-of-season ingredients that have been flown in from the other side of the world. I grew up in the village of Burt, which nestles below the ancient hill fort of Grianán an Aileach and overlooks Lough Swilly and Inch Island. My brothers and I used to trek up to the top of Grianán and then freewheel our bikes all the way down! It was only when I got older that I realised I could put together an entire meal from the fields around my home. These are my favourite hyper-local recipes.

Big, Hearty Veggie Broth

We were reared on vegetable broth, and on the odd occasion some chicken was added! It wasn't that we were hard done by, simply that my mother knew that it provided all the nutrition we needed. And if you're wondering why it tastes better on the second day – well, it's because all the ingredients concentrate as the soup reduces in volume to create that big, hearty veggie broth flavour.

SERVES 4

100 g barley

50 g butter

3 cloves of garlic, crushed

1 onion, peeled and diced

150 g leeks, washed and sliced

150 g carrots, peeled and diced

150 g celery, washed and diced

2 bay leaves

200 g potatoes, peeled and diced

Freshly ground white pepper

2 litres vegetable stock

Handful of chopped fresh parsley

1. Soak the barley in cold water for at least 20 minutes.
2. Melt the butter in a saucepan and sweat the crushed garlic, onion, leeks, carrots and celery with the bay leaves for 5 minutes. Add the potatoes and soaked barley.
3. Season with pepper and cover with the vegetable stock.
4. Bring to the boil and allow to simmer for 20 minutes or until the barley is cooked.
5. Add the parsley and serve piping hot.

BRIAN'S TIP

Replace the vegetable stock with homemade chicken stock, made using a whole chicken. Remove the meat from the carcass and add it to the soup pot to turn your veggie broth into a hearty chicken soup.

Cabbage and Bacon with Parsley Sauce

When I was young, a man would often call to our house with local bacon, and it would always go straight into a pot of water to be cooked. I can still remember the smell of cloves filling the house as it simmered.

The cabbage would come from our neighbour, Willie Callaghan. When I was eleven, I used to sell them for him out of a wheelbarrow that I pushed around our area. His cabbage always had an amazing flavour.

SERVES 4

---

700 g back bacon

1 onion, finely chopped

6 cloves

1 head green savoy cabbage, shredded

Freshly ground black pepper

60 g butter

60 g plain flour

100 ml white wine

150 ml cream

200 ml reserved cooking liquid

Handful of parsley, chopped

1. Place the bacon in the pot with the onion and cloves and cover with cold water.
2. Bring to the boil and simmer gently for 1 hour. Save the cooking liquid for the sauce.
3. Cook the cabbage in boiling water for 12–14 minutes. Drain, season with pepper and set aside.
4. Meanwhile, melt the butter in a saucepan and add the flour. Stir until you have a paste, and cook for 2 minutes.
5. Mix the wine, cream and 200 ml of the cooking liquid from the bacon together. Add slowly to the flour and butter, stirring all the time – the sauce will thicken gradually. Add the chopped parsley to the sauce and leave aside in a warm place.
6. Slice the bacon while warm and serve with the cabbage and a generous amount of the parsley sauce.

BRIAN'S TIP

This is delicious with boiled new potatoes.

Carrots Three Ways

As a child, I was always told to eat my carrots because they were good for my eyesight. Well, guess what, I wear glasses, so clearly I didn't eat enough! Nowadays, they're one of my favourite vegetables because you can have them either hot or cold, as part of a main meal or as a snack. These are my three favourite ways to serve carrots.

ORANGE GLAZED CARROTS

Orange gives carrots a nice tang. Simply peel and slice as many carrots as you need and place in a pot with a knob of butter. Cover with orange juice and a sprinkle of sugar. Cover with a lid and bring to the boil. Then reduce the heat and remove the lid. Cook until liquid has evaporated and the carrots have a nice glaze.

BBQ CARROT CHIPS

A great healthy snack that's easy to prepare and perfect for the barbecue. Peel and cut the carrots like chips. Brush them with melted butter and sprinkle with a twist of black pepper. Place them on the barbecue, turning regularly, until the carrots are cooked. Serve with a dip of crème fraiche with a pinch of chilli powder.

JUICE IT

A shot of carrot juice is great for boosting your immune system and fighting colds and flus. Juice with apples for a tasty carrot and apple juice (3 carrots for every apple). Serve chilled.

BRIAN'S TIP

For added zing, juice a thumbnail-sized piece of root ginger with your carrots and apple.

Roasted Honey and Herb Vegetables

Roasting is the perfect technique for producing great-tasting vegetables on occasions when you have a lot of mouths to feed. I love this recipe because it's guaranteed to produce that all-important crispy texture.

SERVES 4–6

2 sweet potatoes

3 potatoes

2 carrots

½ butternut squash

2 parsnips

2 red onions

4 shallots

4 cloves of garlic

4 tbsp rapeseed oil

Freshly ground black pepper

Pinch of nutmeg

1 sprig of rosemary

2 sprigs of thyme

50 g local honey

1. Place a large flat tray in a hot oven for 15 minutes at 200°C/400°F/Gas Mark 6.

2. Peel and roughly chop the sweet potatoes, potatoes, carrots, butternut squash and parsnip into thick-cut, chip-style shapes. Cut the red onions and shallots into wedges and chop the garlic.

3. Place the vegetables in a bowl and add the oil, black pepper and nutmeg. Add the fresh rosemary and thyme and mix together.

4. Place the vegetables on to the hot tray. You should hear them sizzle immediately.

5. Quickly return the tray to the oven and cook for 30 minutes, shaking the tray halfway through.

6. Drizzle with the honey and return to the hot oven for another 8 minutes, then serve.

BRIAN'S TIPS

Preheating the tray is the secret to always-crispy roasted vegetables. Make sure it's piping hot before you add the veg, and return it to the oven immediately. Any leftovers make a tasty wrap with some mozzarella and basil for lunch the next day.

Turnip, Leek and Potato Soup

I was once given the job of counting turnips on a farm. I'd reached 1100 when I found out it wasn't a real job, just a way to keep me quiet! I never got over it and I still think of it every time I cook with turnips. I love their flavour and when used properly in a soup they really turn it into something special.

SERVES 4–6

50 g butter

200 g small onions, chopped

4 cloves of garlic, crushed

200 g leeks, trimmed and chopped

200 g celery sticks, trimmed and chopped

200 g turnips, peeled and diced

200 g potatoes, peeled and diced

2 litres hot vegetable stock

Sprig of tarragon, chopped

Freshly ground black pepper

150 ml cream

1. Melt the butter in a large saucepan and sweat the onions and garlic in it for a few minutes. Then add the leeks, celery, turnips and potatoes.

2. Sweat for a further 4–5 minutes, stirring all the time, and then add the stock, tarragon and pepper.

3. Simmer for about 15 minutes, until the vegetables are soft, then add the cream and remove from the heat.

4. Blend the soup in a blender and serve piping hot.

BRIAN'S TIP

Try replacing turnip with celeriac for an earthier flavour and creamier texture.

THE LOCAL BUTCHER

Butchers know meat better than anyone, and your local butcher is the key to you and your family eating well. When I'm travelling around Donegal I always make a point of calling in to the local butcher's shop, as I never know what I'll come away with, and it's important to support independent traders – otherwise all their knowledge and expertise will be lost. Your butcher can tell you which cuts work best in which dishes and will always have recommendations or suggestions for new things to try. These recipes are inspired by some of Donegal's best butchers.

Steak with Béarnaise Sauce

I'm often asked what my favourite meal would be. I don't have to think about it, even for a second, as my answer never changes. It has to be steak with Béarnaise sauce.

SERVES 2

For the Béarnaise sauce

2 tsp white wine vinegar

½ shallot, finely chopped

2 egg yolks

120 g butter, melted

Handful of fresh tarragon, chopped

Freshly ground black pepper

Squeeze of fresh lemon juice

For the steak

Drizzle of rapeseed oil

2 Irish sirloin or rib-eye steaks

2 cloves of garlic, sliced

1 fresh rosemary sprig, chopped

2 tomatoes, deseeded and chopped

Sprig of tarragon, chopped

1. To make the sauce, put the vinegar and shallot in a small saucepan and place over a medium heat. Simmer to reduce the liquid by half.

2. Place the egg yolks in a bowl over steaming water and whisk them slowly. Gradually add the warm melted butter, whisking all the time, until all the butter is added and you have a thick, mayonnaise-like consistency.

3. Add the reduced vinegar and shallots and whisk gently to combine. Season with the chopped tarragon and plenty of black pepper, and add a squeeze of lemon juice. Leave aside while you cook the steak.

4. Heat a frying pan until it is smoking hot.

5. Add a drizzle of oil and place the steaks in the pan. Leave them for 2 minutes and then turn.

6. Now add the garlic and rosemary, and season with black pepper. Cook for a further 3 minutes.

7. Allow the steaks to rest for a few minutes off the heat, and then serve with your luxurious Béarnaise sauce, some chopped tomato and a sprinkle of tarragon. Heaven!

BRIAN'S TIP

Resist the urge to agitate the steaks while cooking—poking them will pierce the seal created by the hot pan and you'll lose all your lovely meat juices. Relax and trust yourself to just let them cook—it'll be worth it!

Mammy's Irish Stew

I don't think there is a person in Ireland who hasn't enjoyed an Irish mammy's Irish stew at some point in their lives. For me, Irish stew didn't just taste amazing – it also provided security and comfort as I sat at the table with my mammy. I used to run home from school to beat my brothers in the door and ensure I got a decent portion before them.

SERVES 6

---

1 kg diced Irish lamb (preferably shoulder cut)

2 bay leaves

Drizzle of rapeseed oil

2 cloves of garlic, crushed

1 onion, peeled and diced

1 carrot, peeled and diced

½ leek, diced

1 parsnip, peeled and diced

2 sprigs of fresh thyme

Freshly ground black pepper

4 potatoes, peeled and diced

2 litres warm chicken stock

Handful of young cabbage leaves, chopped

BRIAN'S TIP

Scoop out the inside of a round sourdough bap, leaving just the crust, and serve the stew inside the bread.

1. Cover the lamb pieces in water and simmer with one of the bay leaves for about 20 minutes.
2. Heat a casserole pot, add the oil and sweat the vegetables, starting with the garlic and onion and followed by the carrot, leek and parsnip.
3. Add the sprigs of thyme and the remaining bay leaf. Season with black pepper. Sweat for roughly 5 minutes, stirring all the time, then add the diced potato.
4. Drain the lamb and immediately add the meat to the vegetables. Cover with the warm stock. Put on the lid and simmer for about 1 hour, stirring occasionally.
5. After an hour, add the chopped cabbage and check if the lamb is tender. If not, cook for a further 20 minutes.
6. Serve this hearty dish in a bowl and enjoy with family and friends.

Pork Chops with Toffee Apple

Pork is one of the most underrated meats available. For years it's been served overcooked and, unsurprisingly, that's given it a bad name. When you cook pork properly, you'll find it's succulent and tasty. Trust me: served with toffee apple, it's a treat of a meal in fifteen minutes.

SERVES 4

---

4 pork chops

Drizzle of rapeseed oil

Freshly ground black pepper

4 sprigs of fresh thyme

1 red apple

40 g butter

50 g brown sugar

50 ml water

BRIAN'S TIP

Serve with spinach or cabbage and potatoes for a tasty and affordable dinner party dish.

1. Preheat the oven to 150°C/300°F/Gas Mark 2.
2. Brush the pork chops on both sides with oil and season with the black pepper. Add the sprigs of fresh thyme.
3. Heat a frying pan and fry the chops for 3 minutes on each side until they are golden. Transfer them to a tray and place in the warm oven for 4 minutes.
4. Core the apple, leaving the skin on, and cut into 4 slices.
5. Place the pan you fried the chops in over a medium heat and add the butter. Place the apple slices in the pan and sprinkle with half the brown sugar. Cook for 2 minutes, then turn over and sprinkle the other side with the rest of the sugar. Cook for a further 2 minutes. The sugar will turn a sticky, syrupy consistency. Add the water to the pan and allow the sugar to caramelise.
6. Serve a toffee apple slice on top of each pork chop.

Sunday's Finest Roast Lemon and Thyme Chicken

A roast chicken on a Sunday is simply scrumptious, and the leftovers picked from the bones are just as tasty that evening or the next day. Chicken can be fairly bland but lemon and thyme pack a big punch, which is why they work so well in this recipe.

SERVES 4

---

1 kg whole chicken

Drizzle of rapeseed oil

Freshly ground black pepper

6 sprigs of fresh thyme

1 lemon

6 cloves of garlic

1 onion

2 carrots

100 ml cider or apple juice

BRIAN'S TIP

Any leftover chicken is great in wraps, salads or sandwiches. Roast two chickens and keep one to start the week with great packed lunches or easy dinners at home.

1. Preheat the oven to 190°C/375°F/Gas Mark 5.
2. Brush the skin of the chicken with oil. Season with black pepper and sprinkle with fresh thyme.
3. Zest the lemon and rub the zest around the breasts and legs of the chicken. Cut the zested lemon into slices and place underneath the chicken. Place the garlic cloves inside.
4. Peel the onion and carrots, then slice in half and place in a roasting tray. Set the chicken on top. Add the cider or apple juice to the base of the tray and place in the oven.
5. Roast the chicken for 1 hour. Allow to rest for about 20 minutes, and then slice and serve with the juices from the tray drizzled over the meat.

The Homes of Donegal Cottage Pie

Cottage pie has to be the ultimate comfort food. It's simple – a meat base with gravy and a thick layer of mashed potatoes – and it's the sort of dish that's been served in family homes in Ireland for generations. There's a reason why it's still eaten – and adored – by young and old!

SERVES 4–6

Drizzle of rapeseed oil

500 g minced beef

1 onion, peeled and chopped

2 carrots, peeled and diced

3 cloves of garlic, crushed

150 g mushrooms, sliced

1 bay leaf

40 g plain flour

400 g tinned chopped tomatoes

50 g tomato puree

1 litre beef stock

Drop of Worcestershire sauce

450 g mashed potato

Knob of butter, melted

Freshly ground black pepper

1. Preheat the oven to 180°C/350°F/Gas Mark 4.
2. In a saucepan, heat the rapeseed oil and brown the minced beef, stirring all the time to break up the meat. Add the onion, carrots and garlic, followed by the mushrooms. Then drop in the bay leaf and lightly fry for a further 4–5 minutes.
3. Add the flour and mix thoroughly. Then add the chopped tomatoes and tomato puree, followed by the stock.
4. Allow to simmer for 25 minutes, stirring occasionally. Remove from the heat and season with pepper and a drop of Worcestershire sauce.
5. Heat the mashed potato.
6. Spoon the cottage-pie filling into an earthenware dish and spread a layer of mashed potato on top. Brush with the melted butter, sprinkle with some black pepper and place in the oven for 15 minutes.
7. Serve in warmed bowls.

BRIAN'S TIP

Cottage pie is another great meal for preparing in advance to eat during the week. I like to make individual cottage pies in small dishes and then freeze them.

Marinated Lamb with Slaw

Lamb is meat from a sheep that is less than a year old, and its youth means it has a sweet and succulent flavour. You can use either lamb chops or steaks for this recipe – both cuts are available from your local butcher.

SERVES 4

8 lamb chops or lamb steaks

For the rub

2 cloves of garlic

6 fresh mint leaves

2–3 sprigs fresh rosemary

Freshly ground black pepper

Zest of ½ a lemon

25 ml rapeseed oil

1 tsp wild honey

For the slaw

200 g white cabbage, shredded

200 g red cabbage, shredded

1 red onion, diced

2 carrots, peeled and grated

4 tsp light mayo

Fresh mint leaves

Pinch of chilli flakes

Squeeze of lime juice

Freshly ground black pepper

To serve

2 fresh mint leaves, chopped

RUB

1. Crush the garlic and finely chop the mint and rosemary. Add the pepper, lemon zest and oil and mix together. Then add the honey.

2. Spread the rub over the lamb and leave to marinate for at least 15 minutes.

SLAW

1. Put all the ingredients into a bowl and mix together. Cover with cling film and chill in the fridge.

LAMB

1. Preheat a frying pan. Cook the lamb chops or steaks for 3 minutes on each side, turning halfway through.

2. Serve with chilled slaw on the side. Slice the zested lemon and serve a slice with each chop. Sprinkle with chopped mint leaves

BRIAN'S TIP

Spread the rub on a half leg of lamb – or double the recipe for a full leg of lamb – to make an incredible roast. The meat is also delicious with minted yoghurt (see p. 171) instead of slaw.

Stuffed Beef Olives

Beef olives are basically stuffed beef rolls served with a natural jus. I first tried them when I went to catering college in Killybegs, and I've managed to find my original recipe for them. I've tried lots of variations over the years but, for me, this is a recipe that simply can't be beaten.

SERVES 4

For the stuffing

50 g butter

1 onion, peeled and finely diced

150 g smoked bacon, finely diced

2 cloves of garlic, crushed

10 fresh sage leaves, finely chopped

Pinch of nutmeg

Freshly ground black pepper

50 g fresh breadcrumbs

For the beef

4 topside steaks

20 g flour

Drizzle of rapeseed oil

150 ml red wine

400 ml beef stock

2 sprigs of thyme

1. Preheat the oven to 160°C/325°F/Gas Mark 3.

2. To make the stuffing, melt the butter and sweat the onion with the bacon, garlic and chopped sage leaves for about 4 minutes. Season with nutmeg and pepper and then remove from the heat. Add the breadcrumbs and mix well.

3. Place the steaks between two layers of cling film and beat with a rolling pin to flatten. Remove the cling film, divide the stuffing between the steaks and roll. Secure with butcher's string or a cocktail stick. Roll the stuffed steaks in the flour and pat to remove any excess.

4. Heat a frying pan and add the oil. Fry the stuffed steaks on all sides. Add the red wine and allow it to reduce by half. Then add the stock and pop in the fresh thyme.

5. Transfer to a deep earthenware dish, cover with a lid and cook in the oven for 2½ hours. Serve with the juices from the dish.

BRIAN'S TIP

Brush the beef with mustard prior to stuffing for an extra-peppery flavour.

Sausage and Pasta Bake

Sausages were once considered only a breakfast item, but nowadays, thanks to the skill and innovation of our butchers, the quality and variety of sausages have never been more exciting. It's no wonder gourmet sausages are becoming a popular protein choice for easy midweek meals.

SERVES 4

1 tbsp rapeseed oil

1 onion, peeled and diced

4 mushrooms, sliced

4 sprigs of fresh thyme

Freshly ground black pepper

2 cloves of garlic, chopped

8 thick pork sausages

400 g tomato passata

500 ml hot vegetable stock

300 g penne pasta

10 fresh basil leaves, chopped

50 g breadcrumbs

50 g grated cheese of your choice

1. Preheat the oven to 200°C/400°F/Gas Mark 6.
2. Heat a large frying pan, add the oil and sweat the onion and mushrooms with the thyme and pepper for 3–4 minutes. Add the garlic and cook for 2 more minutes.
3. Cut the sausages into bite-size chunks, add to the pan and fry until coloured on all sides. Add the passata and vegetable stock and season with more black pepper.
4. Simmer gently for 8 minutes.
5. At the same time, cook the penne pasta in boiling water according to the packet instructions. When ready, drain and add to the sausage and tomato mixture.
6. Transfer to an earthenware dish and sprinkle with fresh basil.
7. Mix the breadcrumbs and grated cheese together and lightly sprinkle on top.
8. Bake for 15–20 minutes.

BRIAN'S TIP

Replace the sausages with chicken, bacon or pork pieces for some variety.

Fried Liver and Bacon on Sourdough in Minutes

I bet it's been years since you've had liver – well, the good news is it's making a comeback. It's a super-nutritious meat which is naturally full of iron, and its rich flavour makes it easy to cook with. I love it with these Madeira-infused onions served on toasted sourdough bread.

SERVES 4

---

4 rashers dry-cured bacon

30 g plain flour

Freshly ground black pepper

400 g lamb's liver

Drizzle of rapeseed oil

1 onion, thinly sliced

Splash of Madeira

40 g brown sugar

Knob of butter

4 slices sourdough bread, toasted

1. Grill the bacon until crispy.
2. Mix the flour and pepper, then pat the liver in the flour.
3. Heat a frying pan and fry the sliced onions in the oil. When they've softened, add the Madeira and the sugar. Reduce the heat and cook the onions until they turn slightly sticky.
4. Transfer the onions to a warm place and, using the same pan, add the butter and fry the floured liver for 1–2 minutes on each side.
5. Serve the liver with the crispy bacon and onions on the slices of toasted sourdough.

BRIAN'S TIP

Great with a dollop of ketchup!

Honey-Glazed Donegal Gammon

First things first: gammon is not the same as ham. Gammon is a natural cut, which means the meat is whole muscle, which is much healthier. Gammon used to be soaked prior to cooking to remove the salt but now butchers don't need to use as much salt, as modern packaging preserves the meat, so it's straight into the pot for me. The sweet glaze makes this a real showpiece dish for when you want something to impress at the centre of the table.

SERVES 8

For the gammon

2 kg gammon

1 bay leaf

6 whole cloves

For the glaze

100 g light brown sugar

4 tsp local honey

2 tsp mustard

Pinch of ground cloves

Pinch of nutmeg

Few drops of Worcestershire sauce

1. Place the gammon in a large pot and cover with cold water. Add the bay leaf and cloves. Bring to the boil and allow to simmer for 1½ hours, making sure there is only gentle movement in the water.
2. Turn off the heat and allow the meat to rest for 10 minutes, then remove from the cooking liquid.
3. While the meat is resting, preheat the oven to 200°C/400°F/Gas Mark 6.
4. Make the glaze by combining all the ingredients in a bowl. Place the gammon on a tray and, using a sharp knife, score the fat with crisscross lines (be careful not to cut into the meat below).
5. Spread the glaze over the meat and cook in the oven for a further 20 minutes, basting with juices from the tray once or twice.

BRIAN'S TIP

People often ask me whether they should boil their gammon. Don't! Boiling will toughen the meat. Gentle simmering is the key to tender gammon.

IN DONEGAL WATERS

I love calling down to the pier at Greencastle – it always makes me feel hungry! Seafood doesn't get any fresher than the fish landed there, and I can get it back to my cookery school and in the pan in 15 minutes. It's one of the simplest, quickest and healthiest foods you can cook – and it is literally right there on my doorstep. In Ireland, you're never too far from the sea, and your fishmonger will be able to tell you where the fish you'll use in these recipes has come from.

Middle-of-the-Table Mussels with Dry-Cured Bacon

Mussels are the perfect middle-of-the-table, sharing food experience. I've convinced friends who say they don't eat seafood to try mussels this way and they've been blown away by the flavour. I remember teaching a group of twelve- to fourteen-year-olds who were adamant they did not eat mussels, yet when cooked at the side of the pier in Greencastle they devoured the lot!

SERVES 6

---

4 rashers dry-cured bacon

2 kg Irish mussels

3 cloves of garlic, crushed

1 bay leaf

1 small onion, diced

50 ml white wine

150 ml cream

Freshly ground black pepper

Handful of fresh parsley, chopped

Crusty bread (for dipping)

1. Grill the bacon until crispy, then set aside. Wait until they've cooled, then cut them into strips.
2. Wash the mussels in cold water. Discard any open mussels.
3. Place the mussels, garlic, bay leaf, onion and white wine into a large pot, and cover with a lid. Place on the hob for about 6 minutes, shaking the pot a couple of times during cooking. The mussels should all have opened – remove any that remain closed.
4. Add the cream, pepper and chopped parsley and cook for a further 2 minutes. Remove from the heat and add the strips of bacon.
5. Serve with crusty bread to soak up the scrumptious sauce.

BRIAN'S TIP

I always serve my mussels in the middle of the table in the pot they were cooked in. It looks and smells great, and there's no better way to encourage my guests to get stuck in!

Greencastle Fish Stew

A fish stew is basically a heartier version of chowder. I like to create a really wholesome, creamy texture for my stews by poaching the fish in milk. This captures all the delicious taste of the fish and makes a perfect stock for your stew.

SERVES 6

---

200 g salmon, boned and skinned

200 g Greencastle smoked whiting or haddock, boned and skinned

200 g Greencastle unsmoked haddock, boned and skinned

500 ml milk

2 bay leaves

50 g butter

1 onion, diced

2 cloves of garlic, crushed

2 sticks of celery, peeled and diced

Half a leek, thinly sliced

2 carrots, peeled and diced

Half a bulb of fennel, diced

3 sprigs of thyme

50 g plain flour

Sprinkle of dried dill

2 potatoes, peeled and diced

Freshly ground black pepper

Drop of Worcestershire sauce

Fresh chives or parsley, chopped, to serve

1. Place the boned and skinless fish in a pot and add the milk and 1 bay leaf. Bring to the boil, then reduce the heat and poach for 8 minutes.

2. In a separate pot, melt the butter and sweat the diced onion, crushed garlic, celery, leek, carrots, fennel, remaining bay leaf and sprigs of thyme for 3–4 minutes.

3. Add the flour and mix in thoroughly. Then add the dill.

4. Drain the milk from the fish and add the milk straight in with the vegetables. Add the diced potatoes and stir occasionally.

5. Season with the freshly ground pepper and a drop of Worcestershire sauce and cook for 15 minutes on a low heat, stirring occasionally. The stew will thicken.

6. Add some broken fish pieces to a bowl and serve the stew over them, piping hot.

7. Serve with a sprinkle of fresh chives or parsley

BRIAN'S TIP

This is great with some homemade brown bread.

Grilled John Dory with Savoury Butter

If you're a seafood lover you'll be familiar with John Dory, as it's the tastiest fish ever. Butter is a great Irish ingredient and we should never have reduced its use in our cooking. You can keep this savoury butter to use with any fish dish. I let the ingredients speak for themselves in this recipe.

SERVES 4

For the butter

12 capers

Pinch of fresh dill

1 clove of garlic, chopped

Freshly ground black pepper

250 g butter, softened

1 lemon

Few drops of Worcestershire sauce

12 fresh basil leaves

For the fish

75 g plain flour

Freshly ground black pepper

600 g John Dory fillets

25 g butter, melted

Drizzle of rapeseed oil

BRIAN'S TIP

The butter will keep for three weeks wrapped in the fridge. For a different twist, try adding chopped anchovies to the mixture.

SAVOURY BUTTER

1. Place the capers, dill, garlic and a few twists of pepper into a blender and blitz. Add the softened butter, the zest of the lemon and the Worcestershire sauce and give the mixture a final quick blitz.

2. Chop the basil leaves and sprinkle on a sheet of greaseproof paper. Spread the butter mixture on the paper and roll into a cylindrical shape. Refrigerate for an hour until it hardens.

FISH

1. Heat the grill.

2. Season the flour with pepper. Pat the John Dory fillets in the flour and place on a flat oiled tray.

3. Brush the fish with melted butter and place under the grill for 8 minutes.

4. Remove and place on warmed plates. Cut slices of the butter the thickness of a coin and place 3 slices on each portion of fish. The heat of the John Dory will melt the butter.

5. Add a good squeeze of the zested lemon just before serving.

Pan-Fried Hake with Rosemary, Leeks and a Runny Poached Egg

If you want more fish in your diet then hake is an excellent choice, as it's easy to cook, soft in texture and has far fewer bones than any other fish. It was rarely eaten years ago, but it's now one of my top fish choices.

SERVES 4

Drizzle of rapeseed oil

40 g butter

600 g fresh hake fillets

2 sprigs of rosemary

Freshly ground black pepper

1 lemon

½ leek, sliced

½ onion, sliced

1 clove of garlic, crushed

100 ml cream

4 free-range eggs

1. Heat a frying pan and add a drizzle of rapeseed oil and half the butter. Place the hake in the pan, skin-side down, and cook for 2 minutes. Add the sprigs of rosemary.

2. Turn the hake over, season with black pepper and add the zest of the lemon. Cook on medium heat for 4 minutes, then transfer the fish to a warm tray.

3. Using the same pan, add the rest of the butter, followed by the leek, onion and garlic. Reduce the heat and sweat for 2–3 minutes. Add the cream and allow it to warm through. Season with freshly ground black pepper.

4. While the leeks are sweating, heat some water in a saucepan until light bubbles appear, as in a glass of lemonade. Crack and gently drop the eggs into the water and cook for about 2 minutes, ensuring you retain a soft runny egg.

5. Serve the hake on top of the vegetables and place the poached egg on top. Sprinkle with some more pepper.

BRIAN'S TIP

Try replacing the hake with cod, haddock or turbot.

Wild Atlantic Way Fish Pie

I'm lucky enough to live right on the Wild Atlantic Way. Believe it or not, it's one of the longest coastal routes in Europe, so it seems only fitting to include a dish that celebrates the freshness of the sea. This fresh fish pie tastes so good, I think it should be available in every coastal village along the Wild Atlantic Way.

SERVES 6

---

100 g butter

Bunch of scallions, finely chopped

Freshly ground black pepper

750 g potatoes, cooked and mashed

350 g haddock fillets

350 g smoked haddock fillets

1 bay leaf

500 ml milk

50 g plain flour

100 g local cheese, grated

1 onion, peeled and diced

2 carrots, peeled and diced

White of 1 leek, sliced

4 sticks of celery, diced

50 ml rapeseed oil

4 cloves of garlic, crushed

Handful of fresh parsley, chopped

BRIAN'S TIP

Leftover cooked potatoes work perfectly for this dish. You can also cover your pie with pastry.

1. Melt 50 g of the butter in a pan and sweat the chopped scallions. Mix in through the mashed potato along with a pinch of pepper. Leave aside.

2. Preheat the oven to 200°C/400°F/Gas Mark 6.

3. Place the fish fillets in a pan with the bay leaf and cover with the milk. Bring to the boil and simmer for 7 minutes.

4. Remove the fish from the milk and place in tin foil to keep warm.

5. Melt the remainder of the butter in a saucepan and add the flour to make a roux. Cook for 1 minute. Gradually add the milk the fish was cooked in, and season with pinch of pepper. Stirring all the time, simmer the sauce until it thickens. Add 50 g of the grated cheese.

6. Sweat the onion, carrots, leek and celery in the rapeseed oil until the vegetables have softened.

7. Roughly break up the fish fillets, then place in an ovenproof dish with the vegetables. Pour over the sauce and gently combine. Spread the mashed potato on top and sprinkle with the remaining grated cheese. Bake in the preheated oven for 40 minutes.

8. Allow to rest for 10 minutes before serving. Garnish with chopped parsley.

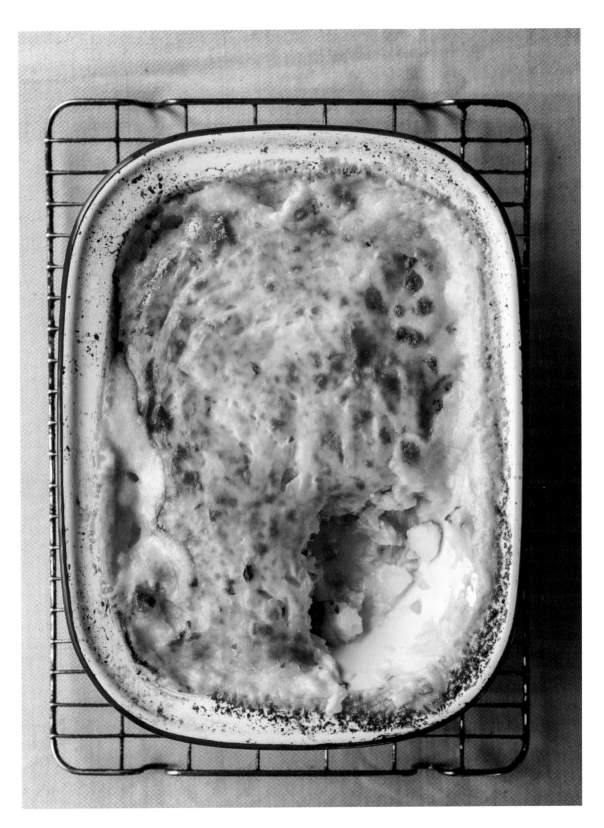

Fried Cod with Greens and Beans

'Chef, I'm afraid of pan-frying cod. What's the secret?' That's a question I'm often asked, and my answer is simple – don't be afraid. All you need is a heated non-stick pan, a drizzle of oil and a knob of butter, and the nerve to leave it and let it cook. The chive and cream cappuccino really brings out the natural flavours of the fish.

SERVES 4

Drizzle of rapeseed oil

50 g butter

2 rashers of smoked bacon, diced

200 g tinned cannellini beans

Half a red chilli, chopped

Handful of green cabbage leaves,
   shredded

Freshly ground black pepper

2 tomatoes, chopped

Handful of spinach leaves

2 scallions, chopped

600 g cod fillets

1 tsp smoked paprika

1 lemon

Sprig of fresh fennel

For the cappuccino

50 ml cream

Handful of chives

1. Heat a frying pan and add a drizzle of rapeseed oil and half the butter. Add the diced smoked bacon and lightly fry until crispy. Then add the cannellini beans and chilli followed by the shredded cabbage and season with black pepper. Reduce the heat and add the tomatoes, spinach and scallions. Stir and leave on a low heat to keep warm.

2. For the cod, heat a non-stick pan, add a drizzle of rapeseed oil and the rest of the butter. Place the cod in the pan, skin-side down, and cook for 2 minutes then turn. Season with the paprika. Cook for a further minute, then add the lemon zest to the fish, followed by a good squeeze of the lemon juice.

3. To make the cappuccino, heat the cream and add the chives. Whizz in a blender to create a foam.

4. Serve the greens and beans in a bowl with the cod on top and a sprig of fresh fennel.

5. Top with the chive and cream cappuccino.

BRIAN'S TIP

There are lots of great variations on this recipe for you to experiment with. Replace the cod with mackerel, salmon or hake, or try using Irish chorizo or black pudding instead of bacon.

Crispy Prawn Dippers

I first tried this dish when I was in Spain and its flavour was immediately unforgettable. Prawns cooked to perfection are one of my all-time pleasures in life.

SERVES 4

2 limes

2 cloves of garlic, sliced

1 small chilli, deseeded and finely chopped

Knob of ginger, peeled and grated

1 tsp turmeric powder

400 g raw, peeled king prawns

75 g cornflour

10 g sesame seeds, toasted

100 ml rapeseed oil

20 g fresh coriander, roughly chopped

100 g crème fraiche

1. Remove the zest of 1 lime and leave aside. Mix the juice of that lime with the garlic, chilli, ginger and turmeric in a large bowl and leave to infuse for a couple of minutes. Pat the prawns dry with kitchen paper, and then place in the lime marinade. Cover and chill for about 30 minutes.

2. Sift the cornflour into a bowl. Add the toasted sesame seeds, then lightly coat half the prawns in the mixture. Heat half of the oil in a large frying pan and fry the coated prawns for about 3 minutes, turning occasionally, until they are just cooked and crispy in texture. Drain on kitchen paper, cover and keep warm. Coat the rest of the prawns in the cornflour and fry in the remaining oil.

3. Garnish with the coriander and serve immediately with slices of the remaining lime.

4. To make the dip, mix the reserved lime zest with the crème fraiche. Serve alongside the prawns.

BRIAN'S TIP

Replace the prawns with monkfish chunks or squid.

Chargrilled Vegetable and Monkfish Kebabs with Couscous

'Greencastle Monkfish, just landed' is the best phone call I can get. I'm only minutes from the pier, and I love racing down to watch the catch coming in and select the best for the day's menu. I enjoy this recipe, as every time I make it guests love its clean, healthy and light style.

SERVES 4

For the kebabs

600 g monkfish tails

1 red pepper

1 yellow pepper

1 courgette

1 red onion

4 wooden skewers

1 lemon, sliced, to serve

Handful of fresh basil leaves,
    chopped, to serve

For the marinade

2 cloves of garlic, sliced

1 lemon, juice and zest

1 red chilli, thinly sliced

Handful of fresh basil leaves

50 ml rapeseed oil

Freshly ground black pepper

For the couscous

240 g couscous

500 ml boiling water

Handful of fresh basil leaves, chopped

1. Cut the monkfish into nugget-size pieces. Cut the pepper into large 2.5 cm pieces and cut the courgette into large rounds. Cut the onion in half and each half into 3 wedges. Thread the cut vegetables and monkfish onto the skewers.

2. Using a pestle and mortar, grind all the marinade ingredients together. Reserve a small amount for serving, then spread the rest over the skewered fish and vegetables.

3. Grill or barbecue the kebabs. Cook for approximately 10 minutes, turning occasionally.

4. Meanwhile, place the couscous in a bowl and add the boiling water. Stir with a fork and add the chopped basil leaves. Cover tightly with cling film and set aside until all the water has been absorbed.

5. Serve the kebabs with the couscous, a slice of lemon, a sprinkle of freshly chopped basil and the reserved marinade.

BRIAN'S TIP

Why not try a few fresh prawns on your kebabs as well?

Donegal Catch

'You may be beautiful but they are keeping my idea on file, in a filing cabinet.' The greatest TV advertisement ever, in my opinion, and to honour it, I'm creating my very own Donegal Catch. I'm making mine healthy by baking them, rather than deep-frying. It doesn't get much better than fresh fish, breaded and eaten with a squeeze of lemon.

SERVES 4

80 g plain flour

Freshly ground black pepper

800 g white fish fillets (I prefer hake but you can use any white fish)

3 eggs, beaten

200 g breadcrumbs

60 g butter

Drizzle of rapeseed oil

1 lemon, cut into wedges

1. Preheat the oven to 200°C/400°F/Gas Mark 6.
2. Season the flour with the pepper and pat the fish fillets in it. Dip the fillets in the beaten egg, making sure to fully coat them, then place them straight into the breadcrumbs. Pat the breadcrumbs gently onto the fish to ensure each fillet is entirely covered.
3. Heat a frying pan and add a drizzle of oil and 15 g of the butter. Place the fish in the pan and fry for 3 minutes on each side. Repeat this process for each fillet, then place them on a tray and bake in the preheated oven for 5 minutes.
4. Serve with lemon wedges for squeezing over.

BRIAN'S TIP

Make them fish-finger shaped for the children or big kids in your life.

Potted Smoked Haddock Mornay

This is perfect for a dinner party, as it can be prepared in advance. Smoking has become popular again and I'm lucky to have some great fish smokeries near me in Donegal. I prefer the natural smoked fish, which looks as if it has a rusted edge rather than the deep-red colour of the dyed version. Your local fishmonger will be able to advise on the best smoked fish.

SERVES 4

600 g smoked haddock fillets

400 ml milk

50 g butter plus an extra 20 g for greasing the dish

50 g plain flour

Pinch of nutmeg

100 g local cheese, grated

50 g breadcrumbs

Handful fresh parsley, chopped

50 g Parmesan cheese, grated

Freshly ground black pepper

1. Place the smoked haddock fillets in a pan and cover with the milk. Bring to the boil and simmer for 7 minutes.
2. Remove the fish from the milk and place in tin foil to keep warm.
3. Melt the butter in a saucepan and add the flour to make a roux. Cook for 2 minutes, then gradually add the milk the fish was cooked in. Season with a pinch of nutmeg and, stirring all the time, simmer the sauce until it thickens. Add the grated local cheese.
4. Heat the grill. Place the fish into a dish – or divide between 4 individual dishes – and pour the Mornay sauce over it. Sprinkle with breadcrumbs, chopped parsley and grated Parmesan. Add a twist of freshly ground black pepper.
5. Cook under the grill until golden brown.

BRIAN'S TIP

Place a layer of spinach under the fish prior to pouring over the Mornay sauce. It gives a lovely peppery flavour and helps to ensure your family eats their greens!

Chef
Brian Mc Dermott

ONE-POT WONDERS

People love one-pot meals as they cut down on the washing up, but I can assure you that's not the only benefit! Stews, casseroles and curries are just some of the wonderful dishes that can be made using a single pot, and cooking everything together is a great way to intensify the flavours. I have a fabulous bright-orange pot that Brenda and I got as a wedding present, and it's the one I still use to this day. Between March and October I travel all over Ireland going to food festivals, and the no-fuss approach of one-pot cooking is perfect for demonstrations. These are some of my most popular tried-and-tested one-pot recipes.

Lamb and Barley Hot Pot

This dish is so simple to make but it's always a real winner. It's healthy and nutritious, but it also has that one-pot comfort-food vibe which never goes wrong, especially in the winter. Give it a go and this recipe will become a firm favourite in your house, I promise.

SERVES 6

---

75 g barley

1 tbsp rapeseed oil

600 g lamb, diced

3 cloves of garlic, sliced

2 small onions, diced

2 bay leaves

3 sprigs of fresh thyme

Freshly ground black pepper

1 carrot, diced

1 parsnip, diced

2 sticks of celery, thinly sliced

1 litre vegetable stock, warmed

4 medium potatoes

Handful of fresh parsley

BRIAN'S TIP

You could also make this using leftover cooked lamb from your Sunday roast, or try replacing lamb with stewing beef and 100 ml of local porter.

1. Preheat the oven to 170°C/325°F/Gas Mark 3.
2. Cook the barley in boiling water for approximately 25 minutes. Drain and leave aside.
3. Heat a casserole dish, add some of the oil and lightly colour the diced lamb. Add the garlic, onions, bay leaves and 2 sprigs of thyme, and sweat for a few minutes.
4. Season with pepper, then add the carrot, parsnip and celery and continue to cook for a further 5 minutes.
5. Add the cooked barley followed by the warmed stock. Cover with a lid and simmer for approximately 40 minutes or until the lamb is tender.
6. While the lamb is cooking, peel and thinly slice the potatoes. Pan fry them in the rest of the oil, turning regularly, until tender. Remove the leaves from the remaining sprig of thyme and sprinkle over the potatoes. Season with pepper.
7. Arrange the potatoes on top of the lamb and replace in the oven for a further 15 minutes.

Beef and Ale Casserole

The emergence of quality local beers and ales means that nowadays this recipe can be 100 per cent local. The ale adds a real bitter flavour to this dish, and it's a perfect winter warmer for the cold nights in. Ask your butcher for a shin of beef to use in this recipe.

SERVES 6

Drizzle of rapeseed oil

1 kg beef shin, cubed

2 onions, diced

4 cloves of garlic, crushed

2 bay leaves

2 carrots, peeled and diced

2 sticks of celery, sliced

25 g tomato puree

25 g plain flour

250 ml local ale

220 ml beef stock

2 sprigs of fresh thyme

Freshly ground black pepper

8 mushrooms, sliced

1. Preheat the oven to 170°C/325°F/Gas Mark 3.

2. Add a drizzle of oil to a casserole pot and brown half of the meat pieces. Remove, then brown the second half.

3. Return all the beef to the pot and add the onions, garlic, bay leaves, carrots and celery and cook for 5 minutes, stirring occasionally.

4. Add the tomato puree and flour and mix well. Then add the ale and stir it through the vegetables and beef. Top it up by adding the beef stock and the sprigs of thyme, and then season with pepper.

5. Add the sliced mushrooms and simmer for 10 minutes. Put on the lid and transfer to the oven for 3 hours, stirring every 30 minutes.

BRIAN'S TIP

Serve with chopped parsley and some mashed potato, or for added comfort-food factor, serve with dumplings.

Pork, Apple and Cider Medley

Pork is a superb meat and goes perfectly with apple and cider. We're lucky that we make some of the best cider in the world in Ireland, and its acidity helps to tenderise the pork as well as enhancing the flavour. It'll cut right through any notions you might have that pork isn't tasty.

SERVES 6

Drizzle of rapeseed oil

600 g pork, diced (fillet is best)

1 onion, diced

2 cloves of garlic, sliced

100 g leeks, sliced

6 fresh sage leaves

200 ml local cider

100 ml cream

1 sweet apple, diced

40 g breadcrumbs

1. Heat a frying pan and add a drizzle of oil. Fry the pork pieces till browned. Add the onion, garlic and leeks and sweat for 4 minutes.

2. Add 4 chopped sage leaves and the cider. Allow the cider to reduce by half. Then add the cream and the diced apple and simmer until the sauce thickens – about 4 minutes.

3. Chop the 2 remaining sage leaves and mix with the breadcrumbs. Sprinkle over the pork. Place under the grill for a few minutes until the breadcrumbs are crisp.

BRIAN'S TIP

For a healthy, nutritionally balanced meal, serve with boiled rice or pasta.

Braised Burt Steak with Caramelised Onions and Gravy

My home village of Burt is a proud place which was once the location of Ireland's largest single farm, Grianán Estate, which nestled under the Neolithic ring fort of Grianán an Aileach. We used to play there as kids, and the lush, green fields produced some of the best ingredients in the country. I remember once that a plane had to be used to spray fertiliser on the fields because the farm was so big. The area still produces great food, including the beef I'm using in this recipe.

SERVES 4

Drizzle of rapeseed oil

4 rump steaks (approximately 100 g each)

2 sprigs of fresh thyme

Freshly ground black pepper

2 onions, sliced

2 cloves of garlic, sliced

50 ml vinegar

2 5g brown sugar

40 g tomato puree

25 g plain flour

350 ml hot beef stock

1. Heat a frying pan and add a drizzle of oil. Fry the steaks for about 3 minutes on each side, and season with fresh thyme and pepper. Leave the steaks aside.

2. In the same pan, add the sliced onions and garlic. Fry until they turn brown, and then add the vinegar and brown sugar. Cook until a slightly sticky consistency is achieved, and then add the tomato puree and flour, followed by the beef stock.

3. Return the steaks and any juices to the pan and simmer for 15 minutes. The sauce will thicken and gather around the steaks like a comfort blanket. If you need to loosen it, add a splash of hot water.

BRIAN'S TIP

This is great served on toasted sourdough, or keep it simple and serve with some good quality champ or poundies (see page 106).

Chicken Thighs with Chorizo and Tomato

Chicken thighs are the tastiest part of the chicken and, even better, they're always cheap to buy. Combine them with Irish-made chorizo and you have the ultimate flavour combination.

SERVES 4

---

4 cloves of garlic, sliced

4 sprigs of fresh thyme

1 lemon

Drizzle of rapeseed oil

Freshly ground black pepper

8 chicken thighs

150 g chorizo, chopped

2 red peppers

8 tomatoes, diced

Handful of fresh basil, chopped

BRIAN'S TIP

For a nutty flavour and some extra crunch, sprinkle with toasted sesame seeds before serving.

1. Preheat the oven to 180°C/350°F/Gas Mark 4.

2. In a bowl, mix the sliced garlic, thyme and the zest and juice of the lemon with the rapeseed oil. Season with black pepper.

3. Cut a slit through the skin in each chicken thigh and place them in a deep earthenware dish. Massage some marinade into each thigh and drizzle the remainder over the whole dish.

4. Place in the oven and cook for 45 minutes, then remove. Scatter the chorizo, peppers and tomatoes in between the chicken thighs and return to the oven for a further 15 minutes.

5. Serve in the baking dish, or remove and serve on a platter, with freshly chopped basil.

Moville Regatta Gathering Pot

Every year Moville's regatta attracts both Irish and international crowds. I always like to leave something on the stove cooking while we go and watch, safe in the knowledge that there'll be enough to feed everyone when we get back. A whole poached chicken with loads of vegetables is perfect for this, as it can serve up to ten people.

SERVES 8–10

1 large (1.8 kg) chicken

3 carrots, peeled and sliced

1 leek, washed and sliced

3 sticks of celery, chopped

2 bay leaves

4 cloves of garlic, sliced

Splash of white wine

Freshly ground black pepper

500 g basmati rice

Handful of fresh parsley, chopped

1. Place all the ingredients, except the rice and parsley, in a large pot and cover with cold water. Bring to the boil, and then reduce the heat to simmer for 1 hour 20 minutes.
2. Remove the chicken and rapidly boil the liquid until it reduces by half.
3. While the liquid is reducing, rinse the rice a couple of times in cold water to remove the starch, and then cook it in 2 litres of boiling water.
4. Remove the meat from the cooked chicken and return it to the liquid to warm through, then serve with the rice and chopped parsley.

BRIAN'S TIP

If you have a big enough pot, cook two chickens at the same time and keep one for sandwiches or wraps for your guests later that evening or the next day.

Lightly Spiced Chicken and Savoury Rice

When I was in India I was taught that the secret to good cooking really is to keep it simple. I love spice in my food, but I know not everyone does, so, to be on the safe side, I'm keeping this dish lightly spiced.

SERVES 4

For the chicken

30 g garam masala

25 ml rapeseed oil

4 chicken breasts (each cut into 4 strips)

1 red onion, thinly sliced

3 cloves of garlic, sliced

Knob of ginger, grated

250 ml coconut milk

350 ml chicken stock, warmed

1 bay leaf

50 g natural yogurt

For the rice

300 g rice

8 cumin seeds

1 bay leaf

4 cardamom pods

To serve

Handful of fresh coriander, chopped

20 g sliced almonds

1. Mix the garam masala in a bowl with the oil. Add the chicken strips and coat with the oil and spice mix. Set aside for 5 minutes.

2. Heat a pan, add a drizzle of oil and lightly fry the red onion, garlic and ginger for 4–5 minutes.

3. Add the chicken, along with all the juices and spices from the bowl. Cook the chicken on both sides until golden. Add the coconut milk, the warm chicken stock and the bay leaf and simmer, stirring occasionally, for 8–10 minutes. Add the yogurt and allow to simmer for a further 2–3 minutes.

4. For the rice, boil a litre of water in a saucepan. Wash the rice in cold water, then place into the boiling water. Add the cumin seeds, bay leaf and cardamom pods. Cook for 8 minutes then drain.

5. Serve the chicken and sauce on a bed of the rice and sprinkle with chopped coriander.

BRIAN'S TIP

If you want more heat, you can add some fresh chilli – but remember who you are cooking for and what heat levels they expect. I like to put chilli oil on the table so that everyone can heat up their dish as they wish.

Chicken and Ham Pie

A good pie was always considered good cooking in our house. I still find it homely when there's pie for dinner, as it encourages chat and social eating. Our dinner table has become the most important space in our house – it's where I hear all the craic from the girls about school, friends and family.

SERVES 10

---

50 g butter

2 carrots, peeled and diced

4 sweet potatoes, peeled and diced

2 onions, diced

2 cloves of garlic, sliced

4 sprigs of fresh thyme

6 chicken breasts, cubed

100 ml white wine

50 g plain flour

750 ml hot chicken stock

300 g cooked ham, cubed

250 ml cream

500 g shortcrust pastry

1 egg, beaten

Handful of fresh parsley, chopped

1. Preheat the oven to 180°C/350°F/Gas Mark 4.
2. In a deep casserole dish, melt the butter and sweat the carrots, potatoes, onions and garlic with half the thyme. Then add the cubed chicken and cook without colouring.
3. Add the wine. Allow to cook for 1 minute then add the flour and stir to combine.
4. Add the stock and allow the sauce to thicken. Add the cooked ham and cream and simmer until the vegetables are soft and chicken is cooked through. Stir frequently.
5. On a floured surface, roll out the pastry to fit your casserole dish.
6. Add the chopped parsley to the pie filling and remove from the heat. Place the pastry on top of the pie and firm in to the edges of the dish. Bake for 30 minutes until golden.

BRIAN'S TIP

Replace the ham with smoked bacon for a deep, smoky flavour.

My Best Ever Veggie Dinner: Early Summer Tart

This dish doesn't even need one pot, just one 25 cm flan tin. I think of it as a challenge to see how many vegetables I can pack in! I've included a recipe to make your own pastry for this. It's actually very easy to make pastry at home and, as you'll find out, it's well worth the effort!

SERVES 8

For the pastry

250 g plain flour

125 g butter, softened, plus a little
    extra for greasing

1 egg

35 ml water

For the filling

Drizzle of rapeseed oil

1 red onion, sliced

2 cloves of garlic, sliced

½ red pepper, diced

2 sprigs of thyme

Freshly ground black pepper

8 sprigs of early sprouting broccoli

Handful of cabbage leaves, chopped

10 cherry tomatoes, halved

90 g cheese of your choice, grated

2 eggs

100 ml cream

1. Preheat the oven to 180°C/350°F/Gas Mark 4.

2. To make the pastry, rub the butter into the flour until it has a sandy, breadcrumb texture. Add the egg and the water and combine to form a firm pastry. Wrap in cling film and allow to rest in the fridge for 20 minutes.

3. Use a little melted butter to grease a 25 cm flan tin.

4. Roll out the pastry and line the tin with it. Place a disc of greaseproof paper on top of the pastry and fill with baking beans.

5. Blind bake the pastry case for 15 minutes.

6. While the pastry is baking, heat a frying pan, add a drizzle of oil and fry the onion, garlic and pepper with sprigs of fresh thyme. Season with black pepper.

BRIAN'S TIP

You can easily change the type of vegetables you use in this recipe to make a whole host of different dinners.

7. Boil some water and cook the broccoli and cabbage in it for 2 minutes, then place in cold water to ensure they stay green.
8. When the pastry is cooked, remove the greaseproof paper and beans and allow it to cool.
9. When the pastry is cool, place half of the cooked vegetables and half of the cherry tomatoes into the pastry case and sprinkle with ⅓ of the grated cheese, then fill up with the remaining vegetables and another ⅓ of the cheese.
10. Whisk the eggs and cream together, season with black pepper and pour into the pastry case on top of the vegetables. Sprinkle with the remaining cheese and bake for 30 minutes.

Fifteen-Minute Orzo Pasta with Bacon and Cabbage

I've fallen in love with orzo pasta. It's easy to cook, looks like rice and allows me to cheat and make a poor man's risotto. This recipe is designed to enable you to cook a tasty dish in fifteen minutes.

SERVES 4

300 g orzo pasta

6 rashers dry-cured bacon

Rapeseed oil

4 cloves of garlic, sliced

2 sprigs of fresh thyme

Freshly ground black pepper

3 leaves cabbage/kale

40 g butter

80 ml cream

80 g Parmesan cheese, grated

To serve

10 g Parmesan cheese, grated

Handful of fresh basil

1. Add the orzo pasta to a pot of boiling water and cook for 8 minutes.
2. While the pasta is cooking, slice the bacon into strips.
3. Heat a drizzle of rapeseed oil in a frying pan then add the garlic followed by the bacon. Cook for a few minutes then drop in the thyme and a sprinkle of black pepper.
4. Roll the washed cabbage or kale leaves and shred. Add to the pan and cook for 2 minutes, then add the butter and cream and simmer for 3 minutes.
5. Drain the pasta and add another drizzle of rapeseed oil. Combine the pasta with the bacon and cabbage or kale in the pot. Add the grated Parmesan and lightly stir.
6. Serve in pasta bowls with more Parmesan and some basil leaves sprinkled on top.

BRIAN'S TIP

For a slightly spicier dish, replace the bacon with chorizo or try adding some diced red peppers and chopped basil.

POUNDIES, SPUDS, POTATOES

Whatever you call them, we do love our potatoes in Donegal. My mum's home was a potato farm, so we were spoilt – in fact, we had so many she always refused to use potatoes that were even a day old! We literally grew up with potatoes, and I think it's fair to say they're still a staple of most of our meals. I like to experiment with them – you can do far more with potatoes than mash or chips! I hope these potato recipes will surprise and inspire you.

Perfect Mash

Rule number one for perfect mash – it must have cream, milk and butter. The next step is to make sure the potatoes are properly cooked – that means until they're soft – and then drained fully to remove excess water. Returning the drained potatoes to the stove for a minute will further dry out the potatoes prior to mashing and help ensure you get perfect mash, every time.

SERVES 4

1 kg potatoes

100 ml milk

75 ml cream

50 g butter

Freshly ground white pepper

Pinch of nutmeg

1. Wash and peel the potatoes, and then cook in boiling water until soft. Drain off the cooking water and return the potatoes to the heat for a minute to allow any remaining moisture to evaporate.
2. In a separate saucepan heat the milk, cream and butter until the butter has melted.
3. Season the potatoes with ground white pepper and nutmeg, then mash.
4. When the potatoes are mashed, add the liquid and return the potatoes to the heat. Keep mashing constantly until you have no lumps.
5. You should now have perfect mash.

BRIAN'S TIP

Add some grated cheese for cheesy mash.

Poundies v. Champ

Poundies are the same as champ, but growing up in Donegal, everyone's mammy made poundies. For me, coming home from school to a plate of poundies is a stand-out memory of home-cooked food.

SERVES 4

---

1 kg potatoes, peeled

50 g butter

6 scallions, sliced

100 ml milk

75 ml cream

Freshly ground white pepper

Pinch of nutmeg

1. Wash and peel the potatoes, then cook in boiling water until soft. Drain off the cooking water and return the potatoes to the heat for a minute to allow any remaining moisture to evaporate.

2. In a separate saucepan, melt the butter with the scallions until the mixture sweats. Cook for 2 minutes, then add the milk and cream and allow the liquid to warm.

3. Season the potatoes with ground white pepper and nutmeg, then mash. When all the potatoes are mashed, add the liquid and return the potatoes to the heat. Keep mashing constantly until you have no lumps.

BRIAN'S TIP

Turn any leftover poundies into potato cakes by shaping them into rounds and pan-frying them in butter.

Savoury Bacon and Leek Potatoes

Bacon and leek is one of my all-time favourite combinations, and when added to potatoes, that flavour combines with the creamy texture to deliver an unbeatable rich taste.

SERVES 4

1 kg potatoes, peeled and thinly sliced

4 rashers of streaky bacon, chopped

600 ml hot vegetable or chicken stock

2 leeks, thinly sliced

25 g butter, for greasing dish

75 ml cream

Freshly ground black pepper

1. Preheat the oven to 200°C/400°F/Gas Mark 6.
2. Place the potatoes in a pot, add the bacon and leeks, cover with hot stock and bring to the boil.
3. Simmer for 6 minutes. Add the cream and season with freshly ground black pepper.
4. Brush a deep ovenproof dish with the butter and add the potato, bacon and leeks.
5. Cover with tin foil and bake for 40 minutes, uncovering halfway through so that any bacon on top crisps up.

BRIAN'S TIP

Add some grated cheese on top of the final layer for a scrumptious, bubbly topping.

Coddle

While coddle is associated with Dublin, we have a strong fondness for it here in Donegal too. When I first had it, the sausages tended to be salty, whereas now, with premium sausages available from your local butcher, this dish has transformed into a quality meal that's still affordable.

SERVES 4

Drizzle of rapeseed oil

450 g sausages

200 g bacon, cut into strips

1 onion, diced

2 carrots, sliced

1 kg potatoes, peeled and sliced

Freshly ground black pepper

500 ml chicken stock, warmed

1 bay leaf

Handful of fresh parsley, chopped

1. Preheat the oven to 170°C/325°F/Gas Mark 3.
2. Heat the oil in a frying pan and brown the sausages. Add the bacon and cook for 2 minutes.
3. Place half of the bacon and sausages in the bottom of an earthenware dish and add half the onions, carrots and potatoes.
4. Season with pepper, and repeat with another layer of meat and vegetables. Pour the warm stock over and add the bay leaf.
5. Cover with a lid and cook for 2 hours. Remove the lid and cook for a further 30 minutes.
6. When cooked, sprinkle with chopped parsley and serve.

BRIAN'S TIP

This is a great recipe to prepare in advance of a family occasion or dinner party. Simply reheat in the oven to serve.

Dauphinoise

I knew how to make this dish before I was able to pronounce it. I first learned it at catering college in Killybegs in the early nineties and I've loved it ever since. It's a classic but easy to make and tastes great with steak and many other meats.

SERVES 4

4 cloves of garlic

500 ml cream

1 kg potatoes, sliced

Freshly ground black pepper

150 g Cheddar cheese, grated

1. Preheat the oven to 160°C/325°F/Gas Mark 3.
2. Peel and slice the garlic and place in a saucepan. Add the cream. Heat and allow to simmer for 5 minutes.
3. In the meantime, slice the potatoes into thin slices about 3 mm thick.
4. Place a layer of potatoes in an earthenware dish and season with pepper. Repeat until all the potatoes are used.
5. Sieve the cream over the potatoes, removing the garlic slices. Sprinkle the cheese on top.
6. Cover with a lid or tin foil, then cook for 1½ hours. Remove the lid or tin foil and cook for a further 20 minutes.
7. Allow to rest for 15 minutes before serving.

BRIAN'S TIP

Sprinkle cheese in between each layer of potato for a super cheesy flavour.

Colcannon

This dish is so good it's almost a meal in itself. My mother made this for me regularly, and before I was tall enough to see into the pot, I can remember the delightful aroma of it filling the kitchen. With the renewed popularity of kale, you can find colcannon on many menus, but after trying this once, I'm sure you'll want to make it a regular feature of your own home cooking.

SERVES 4

---

1 kg potatoes

100 g butter

250 g curly kale, finely sliced

Freshly ground black pepper

100 ml milk, warmed

1. Cook the potatoes in boiling water for 15 minutes or until tender.
2. To cook the kale, heat a knob of the butter in a saucepan and cook the kale in it for 2 minutes. Season with pepper.
3. Drain the potatoes, add in the milk and mash until smooth. Then beat in the kale and the remaining butter.

BRIAN'S TIP

If young kale leaves are not available, use cabbage leaves. Simply cook the cabbage first by boiling it, and then proceed as above.

Baked and Wedged

A bad baked potato is always disappointing, but a good one is memorable. That's why I have included this simple yet effective recipe. Once baked, you can cut them into wedges and serve with toppings as a healthy snack.

SERVES 8

8 large baking potatoes (Roosters are my favourite)

40 ml rapeseed oil, plus extra for wedges

Freshly ground black pepper

8 sprigs of fresh thyme

80 g butter

Handful of fresh chives, chopped

BRIAN'S TIP

If not serving baked potatoes immediately, remove them from the tin foil to avoid sweating.

BAKED POTATOES

1. Preheat your oven to 170°C/325°F/Gas Mark 3.
2. Scrub the potatoes clean, and pierce them with a fork. Brush them with rapeseed oil and season with black pepper. Wrap each one in tin foil with a sprig of thyme and place them all on a tray.
3. Bake for 90 minutes.
4. Once cooked, cut through the tin foil to make a cross on the top and add a knob of the butter and a sprinkle of chopped chives to each.
5. Serve with salads, meats or simply on their own.

POTATO WEDGES

1. Preheat the oven to 180°C/350°F/Gas Mark 4.
2. Cut the cooked baked potatoes in half and then each half into 4 wedges. Drizzle with a little extra rapeseed oil and season with pepper. Place on a tray and return to the oven for 8 minutes.
3. Serve with bacon and cheese, sour cream and scallions or barbecue sauce (see page 179).

Boxty

This mainly Ulster dish has made a great comeback in recent years and rightly so. Rosti, which is a similar dish, has been produced in restaurants for years, but traditional boxty with buttermilk is a much more flavoursome Irish version, still very much alive in the homes of Donegal.

MAKES 8

1 kg potatoes

320 ml buttermilk

160 g plain flour

1 tbsp sugar

¼ tsp bread soda

140 g butter

BRIAN'S TIP

Serve with grilled bacon and a poached egg for one of the greatest breakfasts ever. Or make a large one the size of a frying pan and top with eggs, tomato and honey.

1. Grate the potatoes and place in a clean tea towel. Squeeze all the water out of the potatoes, then place in a large bowl.

2. Immediately pour 270 ml of the buttermilk onto the potato to prevent it from discolouring. Add the flour with the sugar and mix into the potato and buttermilk until you have a thick batter consistency.

3. Dissolve the bread soda in the remaining 50 ml of buttermilk, add to the mix and combine well.

4. Heat a large frying pan and melt 50 g of butter on a medium heat. Add 4 good spoonfuls of the potato mix, leaving some space between them, and cook for 3 minutes on each side or until golden brown. Repeat with another 50 g of butter and the rest of the potato mix.

5. Serve with the remaining butter on top and some slices of Honey-Glazed Donegal Gammon (see page 59) and a dollop of ketchup.

Potato Farls

This is a great dish for using up leftover mashed potatoes, and it's perfect for breakfast or as a snack or side dish with any main meal. If you have guests from overseas, make sure you introduce them to these farls. They'll never underestimate the humble potato again.

MAKES 8

---

75 g plain flour, plus a bit extra for
    dusting

¼ tsp baking powder

Pinch of nutmeg

Freshly ground black pepper

500 g cooked potatoes, mashed

150 g butter, plus extra for serving

BRIAN'S TIP

Add some cheese and bacon and serve with a poached egg for a quick weekend breakfast.

1. Sift the flour with the baking powder and add the nutmeg and some freshly ground black pepper. Add in to your leftover cooked mashed potatoes and stir to combine. It should form a dough.

2. Divide the dough into two halves. Form one piece into a ball, then roll out on a floured surface to create a rough circle about 15 cm in diameter and 5 mm thick. Cut the circle into quarters.

3. Heat a non-stick shallow frying pan over a medium heat with 75 g butter to grease the surface. Transfer the quarters to the pan and cook for about 3 minutes or until golden brown. Flip over and cook the other side for another 3 minutes.

4. Remove to a warm plate, and repeat the process with another 75 g of butter and the other half of the dough mix.

5. Brush with a little more melted butter before serving.

Scalloped

If you ever attended a wedding in a hotel in Ballyliffin in the eighties or nineties you definitely ate scalloped potatoes with your main meal. Occasionally, I still make this dish for visitors to our Donegal home.

SERVES 8

80 g butter, plus extra for greasing
and drizzling

1 onion, finely chopped

80 g plain flour

Freshly ground black pepper

500 ml milk

1 kg potatoes, peeled and thinly sliced

Handful of fresh parsley, chopped

BRIAN'S TIP

Try replacing half the potatoes with sweet potato for a tasty and colourful dish.

1. Preheat the oven to 170°C/325°F/Gas Mark 3. Grease a casserole dish with some melted butter.

2. In a saucepan, melt the 80 g of butter and sweat the onions in it for 4 minutes. Stir in the flour and pepper. Cook, stirring constantly, until smooth, then stir in the milk. Continue to cook, stirring all the time, until the sauce thickens.

3. Layer the potatoes in the casserole dish, and then pour the sauce over them and drizzle over a little more melted butter.

4. Cover with a lid or tin foil and bake for 1 hour or until the potatoes are tender. Remove the lid or tin foil and bake for a further 15 minutes.

5. Allow to stand for 5 to 10 minutes before serving. Serve with freshly chopped parsley

BREAD IN DONEGAL

Nothing takes me back to my childhood more than bread. There's just something about that smell of bread baking when you come in the door, especially when it's cold or wet outside, that takes me right back to Mum's kitchen. She always had something in the oven, usually a soda or scone in case the neighbours called in. Having freshly baked bread ready was always an important part of Donegal hospitality, and it's one of those traditions I try to keep going. These are the bread recipes – and the stories behind them – that I still use to this day.

Scones Three Ways

When I was at secondary school in Scoil Mhuire in Buncrana I had a stint in the convent (not by choice – more through my own misbehaviour!) and every morning began with Sister Enda showing me how to make scones. I hated it then, but, looking back, it was actually one of the best baking lesson I've ever received. I now think of the nuns every time I make scones and thank them for passing on their skills.

MAKES 18

Brian's basic scone recipe

225 g self-raising flour

25 g caster sugar

55 g butter, softened

150 ml buttermilk

1 egg, beaten

1. Preheat the oven to 220°C/425°F/Gas Mark 7. Lightly grease a baking sheet.
2. Sieve the flour into a bowl and add the sugar. Rub the butter into the flour, then stir in the buttermilk to form a soft dough.
3. Turn out on to a floured work surface and knead very lightly.
4. Pat out until the mixture is about 2 cm thick. Use a 5 cm cutter to stamp out rounds and place on the greased baking sheet.
5. Brush the tops of the scones with the beaten egg. Bake for 12–15 minutes until well risen and golden.
6. Cool on a wire rack and serve with local butter and good quality jam and cream for a real treat.

IRISH BERRY

Add 50 g each of chopped raspberries and strawberries for an Irish berry scone.

APPLE AND BLUEBERRY

Add 50 g each of peeled, grated apples and chopped blueberries for an autumn treat.

CHEESE AND SCALLION

Add 40 g grated cheese and 2 chopped scallions to the recipe for a savoury scone.

BRIAN'S TIP

Replace half the flour with mashed potato or potato flour for a great-tasting breakfast or savoury dish.

Barmbrack

Barmbrack is a traditional Irish bake. A coin or a ring is supposed to be hidden somewhere in the mixture, and whoever finds it will have good luck. It was always eaten at Hallowe'en but nowadays it's enjoyed all year round. I find it's one of those recipes that tastes better the next day, so I make my barmbrack a day in advance and wrap it in a tea towel overnight.

MAKES ONE 20 cm CAKE

275 g raisins

100 g sultanas

60 g mixed peel

300 ml warm, strong black tea

50 g treacle

2 apples, peeled and grated

200 g dark brown demerara sugar

225 g self-raising flour

¼ teaspoon mixed spice

1 egg

1. Mix the dried fruit, mixed peel, warm tea and treacle in a bowl. Add the grated apples. Cover with cling film and soak overnight.

2. The next day, preheat the oven to 180°C/350°F/Gas Mark 4. Grease and line a 20 cm round cake tin.

3. Add the brown sugar, self-raising flour, mixed spice and egg to the fruit and tea mixture, then stir well until mixed.

4. Pour into the prepared tin and bake for 1½ hours or until it's firm to the touch.

5. Remove from the tin and allow to cool.

BRIAN'S TIP

Hide a coin or ring in the centre of the cake prior to baking. Wrap in greaseproof paper before inserting in the mixture.

Bacon and Cheese Soda Bread

There's something about the smell of fresh soda bread in a Donegal home, and we need to keep this baking skill alive. I've made this soda bread recipe a bit more exciting with the wonderful combination of flavours that is bacon and cheese.

MAKES ONE LARGE LOAF

---

3 rashers dry-cured bacon, finely
    chopped

225 g self-raising flour

100 g strong cheese, grated

40 g butter

100 ml buttermilk

1. Preheat the oven to 190°C/375°F/Gas Mark 5. Lightly grease a baking tray.
2. Fry the bacon on a dry, hot pan.
3. Sieve the flour into a bowl and add the grated cheese and bacon.
4. Melt the butter and add to the buttermilk. Pour into the flour mix and form a dough by gently mixing.
5. Turn out onto a floured surface and gently shape into a round. Cut a cross on top of the bread and transfer it to the greased baking tray.
6. Bake for 40 minutes.
7. Allow to cool before slicing and serve with real Irish butter.

BRIAN'S TIP

Store in an airtight container. For a warm breakfast option, toast a slice and serve with poached eggs.

Thick Batch Loaf

Fresh bread is bread baked that day, and that's the only way bread used to be eaten. I often ask myself whatever happened to bread baked locally and eaten locally? Quality bread and local butter is seriously good with a cuppa, and many a person's issues have been sorted out over a slice of batch loaf at a Donegal kitchen table!

MAKES ONE 900 G LOAF

---

500 g strong white bread flour

14 g/2 sachets fast-action dried yeast

40 g butter, melted

300 ml lukewarm water

Drizzle of rapeseed oil

BRIAN'S TIP

Brush the top of the bread with a water and sugar syrup for a rich, dark crust.

1. Put the flour and yeast into a large mixing bowl. Add the melted butter to the water and mix to form a dough.

2. Turn the dough out onto a floured table and knead for 4–5 minutes until smooth.

3. Grease a bowl with the oil, place the dough in the bowl and cover it with cling film. Leave in a warm place until the dough has doubled in size – about 1 hour.

4. Preheat the oven to 190°C/375°F/Gas Mark 5. Grease a 900 g loaf tin.

5. Knock the dough back down and knead to form a loaf shape the size of your tin.

6. Place the dough in the greased tin. Cover with cling film and again leave in a warm place until it has more than doubled in size – about 45 minutes.

7. Bake the bread for 45 minutes. Remove from the tin and allow to cool.

8. Cut in thick slices, lather with butter and serve with a cup of tea.

Traditional Hot Cross Buns

Freshly baked hot cross buns are an Easter must for my family. Apparently, if you put hot cross buns in your roof rafters, they'll expel bad spirits and stay fresh until the following year!

MAKES 12

500 g strong white bread flour

7 g/1 sachet fast-action dried yeast

50 g sugar

325 ml milk

40 g butter

1 egg

70 g mixed peel

1 apple, peeled and finely chopped

1 orange, zest only

1 tsp cinnamon

For the cross

50 g flour

For glazing

120 g apricot jam

BRIAN'S TIP

If you prefer, you can include more chopped apples and less mixed peel in this recipe.

1. Sieve the flour into a bowl, and add the yeast and sugar.
2. In a saucepan, bring the milk to the boil and add the butter to it.
3. Make a well in the centre of the flour mixture. Add the warm milk and butter and the egg and combine.
4. Turn the dough out onto a floured surface and knead till smooth. Place the dough in an oiled bowl and cover with a tea towel. Leave in a warm area for about 1 hour until it doubles in size.
5. Preheat the oven to 220°C/425°F/Gas Mark 7.
6. Knock the dough back and add the mixed peel, apple, orange zest and cinnamon to the dough. Mix in well, then turn the dough out onto a floured surface.
7. Divide the dough into 12 even pieces. Shape each one into a ball and place on a lined baking tray.
8. Cover with a tea towel and place in the same warm area to allow it to double in size again – about another hour.
9. To make the cross, simply add a little water to the flour to form a sticky, batter-like consistency. Place the batter in a piping bag and pipe a cross on top of each bun prior to baking.
10. Bake for 20 minutes.
11. Warm some apricot jam, brush over each cooked bun and enjoy!

MY HOME BAKERY

You can buy incredible cakes and treats in the shops these days, but there's still nothing quite like home baking. I've always guarded my dessert recipes fiercely, and I think it's because, out of all the cooking I do, baking is the one that feels the most personal. The ingredients are often very simple – flour, butter, sugar and eggs – but everyone has their own technique that makes their baking style almost like a signature. These are my secret recipes to help you master the perfect cakes and sweets.

Harvest Celebration Carrot Cake

I've been making this cake for years, and I love it because it always reminds me of harvest time in late autumn when you can pack the recipe with carrots and apples. The end of harvest is about marking the end of the year on the farm as the crops are gathered in before winter. A slice of this harvest cake will make you feel part of that time of celebration across rural Ireland.

MAKES ONE 20 CM ROUND CAKE

---

5 eggs

500 g sugar

420 g plain flour

2 tsp bicarbonate of soda

2 tsp cinnamon

1 tsp allspice

420 ml rapeseed oil

500 g carrots, grated

120 g walnuts, chopped

3 sweet apples, peeled and diced

For the icing

140 g icing sugar

100 g butter, softened

220 g cream cheese

1 orange, zest only

To decorate

50 g walnuts, chopped

1. Preheat the oven to 170°C/325°F/Gas Mark 3. Line a 20 cm round cake tin with greaseproof paper.
2. Whisk the eggs and sugar in an electric mixer until light.
3. Sieve the flour and combine with the bicarbonate of soda, cinnamon and allspice.
4. Gently fold the flour and spices into the egg and sugar mix. When combined, add the oil and gently fold through the mix too.
5. Add the grated carrots, walnuts and apple and combine.
6. Spoon the cake mix into the tin and bake for 1 hour 20 minutes. Remove from the tin and place on a cooling rack. Allow to cool completely before decorating.
7. To make the icing, simply combine the icing sugar, butter and cheese in a mixer. When soft and spreadable, add the zest of half the orange.
8. Split the cake in half lengthways, spread a thin layer of the icing and replace the top half of the cake. Spread the remaining icing on the top.
9. Sprinkle some chopped walnuts and the remaining orange zest on top.

BRIAN'S TIP

Try making this recipe in individual
muffin cases for sneaky little treats.

After-School Jam Sponge

If your children have friends coming round after school or a birthday party then this cake is perfect for getting them all gathered round the table. It's also great for taking outside and enjoying as part of a picnic.

MAKES ONE 20 CM ROUND CAKE

200 g butter, softened

200 g caster sugar

4 eggs

200 g self-raising flour

1 tsp baking powder

Few drops vanilla essence

To decorate

150 g strawberry jam

250 ml whipped cream

24 fresh strawberries

Icing sugar, for dusting

BRIAN'S TIP

To help the strawberries stay on the cake, brush the top with a thin layer of strawberry jam first.

1. Preheat the oven to 190°C/375°F/Gas Mark 5. Grease a 20 cm round tin and line with greaseproof paper.
2. Using an electric mixer, cream together the butter and sugar in a bowl. Then add the eggs one at a time, mixing between each addition.
3. Sieve the flour and baking powder and fold into the cake mix. Add the vanilla essence and combine gently.
4. Pour the cake mixture into the tin and bake for 35 to 40 minutes.
5. Remove from the tin and allow to cool. Split the cake in half and spread a layer of jam on the bottom half and then a layer of whipped cream. Put the other half of the cake on top.
6. Decorate with fresh strawberries and dust with sieved icing sugar.
7. Keep refrigerated, as this recipe uses fresh cream.

Celtic Shortbread Biscuits with Strawberries and Cream

I thought I knew about strawberries until I met Pat Clarke. Pat is one of Ireland's leading soft fruit growers and an expert in strawberries. His fruit is simply exceptional. Shortbread with strawberries and cream is as good a treat as you will get anywhere.

MAKES 12

125 g caster sugar

250 g butter, softened

350 g plain flour

100 g semolina

To serve

150 ml fresh cream, whipped

1 punnet of strawberries, sliced

Dusting of icing sugar

BRIAN'S TIP

Add a dollop of strawberry jam before the cream for an even fruitier flavour.

1. Preheat the oven to 180°C/350°F/Gas Mark 4. Line a baking tray with parchment paper.
2. Cream 100 g sugar and the butter together in a bowl using an electric mixer. Sieve the flour into the bowl and add the semolina. Using a wooden spoon, fold together to form a dough.
3. Turn the dough out onto a floured surface and knead gently. Then wrap in cling film and place in the fridge for 20 minutes to rest and chill.
4. Roll the dough out to about 75 mm thick. Cut into desired shapes (I use a 6 cm round cutter) and place on the lined baking tray. Sprinkle with the remaining 25 g sugar and bake for 15 minutes.
5. Remove from the tray and cool on a wire rack.
6. Serve with whipped cream and sliced strawberries and dust with icing sugar.

My Garden Rhubarb Crumble

I only started growing my own rhubarb a few years ago, but it's well worth it. From a four-foot-square plot I can get enough rhubarb to last me all year. I freeze it, stew it and even make jam with it. I love to be able to eat my own rhubarb even when there's snow on the ground outside.

SERVES 4

150 g self-raising flour

50 g light brown sugar

100 g butter, softened

50 g porridge oats

500 g rhubarb, washed and cut into chunks

100 g caster sugar

1 vanilla pod

1. Preheat the oven to 200°C/400°F/Gas Mark 6.

2. For the crumble, mix the flour and brown sugar together and rub in the softened butter until you have a sandy, crumbly texture. Add the porridge oats and gently mix.

3. Spread the crumble out on a tray and bake for 20 minutes until golden brown, stirring halfway through. Set aside to cool.

4. For the rhubarb, simply add it to a pot with the caster sugar and the seeds from the vanilla pod – or use a few drops of good quality vanilla extract.

5. Stew the rhubarb by simmering it for about 15 minutes. Allow to cool slightly.

6. Divide the rhubarb between four 8 cm round dishes. Scatter the crumble on top and place in the oven for 10 minutes. Serve piping hot.

BRIAN'S TIP

You have to serve this with custard and ice-cream, mmm ...

Lemon Drizzle Cake with Summer Berries

Who doesn't love lemon drizzle cake? Well, believe it or not, it's actually easier than you might think to create this wonderful treat. During one of my demos I taught a guy who had never baked in his life how to make this cake live on stage at the Taste of Donegal festival. He went home one very happy man! So what are you waiting for, folks? Have a go!

MAKES ONE 25 CM ROUND CAKE

---

225 g unsalted butter, softened

225 g caster sugar

4 eggs

225 g self-raising flour, sieved

Drizzle of vanilla essence

Zest of 1 lemon, finely grated

For the drizzle topping

Juice of 1 lemon

120 g icing sugar

To garnish

18 raspberries

10 strawberries

20 redcurrants

1. Preheat the oven to 180°C/350°F/Gas Mark 4. Line a 25 cm round tin with parchment paper.

2. In a bowl, beat the butter and caster sugar using an electric mixer until creamy and light in colour.

3. Add the eggs one at a time, mixing between each addition, followed by the sieved flour. Then add the vanilla and lemon zest. Mix well.

4. Spoon the mixture into the tin and bake in the oven for 40–45 minutes.

5. Prepare the drizzle by adding the lemon juice to the icing sugar.

6. Remove the cake from the tin and allow to cool on a wire rack, then drizzle with the icing. Arrange the berries on top.

BRIAN'S TIP

Enjoy with a dollop of freshly whipped cream.

Rustic Irish Apple Pie

I must have robbed every orchard in Bridgend and Burt. Of course, as twelve-year-olds it was all about the excitement of nicking the apples and not getting caught – once we got the apples we hadn't a clue what to do with them! I certainly didn't realise how sought after an item a locally grown apple actually was. For me, the best way to enjoy them is in a traditional apple pie. Anyone who trained as a chef in Killybegs will know this pastry recipe, as it was embedded in our training – and rightly so, because it never fails.

MAKES ONE 20 CM APPLE PIE

250 g plain flour

70 g sugar

125 g butter, softened

2 eggs

4 cooking apples, peeled and sliced

50 g sugar

1 tsp ground cinnamon

Icing sugar to dust

BRIAN'S TIP

Add 100 g of blueberries or strawberries for an alternative flavour. Or try baking in a 25 cm square tin and cut into little squares for afternoon tea or supper.

1. Sieve the flour into a bowl, then add the sugar and mix together. Rub in the softened butter until you have a sandy texture. Add 1 whole egg and combine to form a pastry. Knead and shape into a fat disc. Then chill for 20 minutes.
2. Preheat the oven to 170°C/325°F/Gas Mark 3. Grease a 20 cm pie tin or plate.
3. Beat the remaining egg.
4. Roll the pastry out thinly and place on the tin or plate. Add the sliced apples, then sprinkle with cinnamon and sugar.
5. Roll out the pastry lid and use some beaten egg to seal it to the edge of the pastry base. Brush with more beaten egg and bake for 40 minutes.
6. Remove from the oven and sprinkle with icing sugar.
7. Serve with a dollop of freshly whipped cream.

Easy Chocolate and Raspberry Beetroot Cake with Crème Fraiche

'Beetroot in a cake?' I hear you ask. Yes, and it adds a gorgeous velvety texture as well as a complementary flavour. There's also the added bonus that beetroot is a great healthy 'superfood' so you don't have to feel too guilty about indulging in all that chocolate!

MAKES ONE LOAF CAKE

100 g dark chocolate

150 g cooked beetroot (not in vinegar)

50 ml rapeseed oil

100 g melted butter

3 large eggs

1 tsp vanilla extract

60 g cocoa powder

220 g self-raising flour

200 g caster sugar

100 g fresh raspberries

To decorate

Handful of fresh raspberries

50 g white chocolate

A mint leaf

Dusting of icing sugar

100 g crème fraiche

BRIAN'S TIP

Cook in a small roasting tin and serve with fresh cream as an afternoon tray bake.

1. Preheat your oven to 180°C/350°F/Gas Mark 4. Grease and line a 900 g loaf tin.

2. Melt the dark chocolate in a glass bowl over a saucepan of simmering water.

3. In a blender, blitz the beetroot to a puree. Add the oil and melted butter, then the eggs and vanilla extract. The mix will look pink but, trust me, that's normal.

4. In a large bowl, sieve the cocoa powder and flour, and add in the sugar.

5. Add the pureed mix to the bowl and combine gently together. Stir in the melted chocolate and the whole raspberries.

6. Pour the mix into the lined tin and bake for about 40 minutes. Allow the cake to cool.

7. Decorate the cake with whole raspberries and grated white chocolate, or melt the white chocolate and drizzle over the raspberries. Pop the mint leaf on top and dust with icing sugar.

8. Serve with dollops of crème fraiche.

Five-Minute Ice-Creams

Quick, tasty ice-cream at home is as simple as freezing some good quality fruit. I recommend slicing the fruit and laying it out on a tray lined with cling film, then wrapping the entire tray in cling film until the fruit freezes solid overnight. Once it's safely stored in the freezer, you know you can have ice-cream at any time. I've used berries for these recipes but feel free to experiment with all kinds of fruit.

SERVES 4

STRAWBERRY ICE-CREAM

300 g frozen strawberries

100 g icing sugar

150 ml cream

Place the frozen strawberries in a blender with the icing sugar and cream and blitz until combined. Serve immediately.

BRIAN'S TIP

Add a splash of Prosecco or champagne for an adult version of this ice-cream.

MIXED BERRY ICE-CREAM

150 g frozen strawberries

150 g frozen raspberries

75 g blackberries

100 g icing sugar

150 ml cream

Place the frozen strawberries, raspberries and blackberries in a blender with the icing sugar and cream and blitz until combined. Serve immediately.

BRIAN'S TIP

Line a loaf tin with cling film, spoon the ice-cream into the tin and return to the freezer for at least one hour. Simply slice the ice-cream to serve.

Toffee, Hazelnut and Meringue Roulade

This simple, tasty recipe for my version of a meringue roulade is a must try, and once you master making and folding the roulade, you can fill it with fruits, jams and creams of your choice. I've gone for a sticky toffee flavour in this recipe to be indulgent. Why not?

SERVES 10

For the roulade

75 g hazelnuts, roughly chopped

5 egg whites

275 g caster sugar

Drop of vanilla paste

For the toffee sauce

150 g Demerara sugar

150 g butter, diced

350 ml cream

50 g golden syrup

For the filling

250 ml cream

Drop of vanilla paste

50 g toffee sauce

To decorate

30 g icing sugar, for dusting

Handful of mint leaves

1. Preheat the oven to 200°C/400°F/Gas Mark 6.
2. Line a Swiss-roll tin with greaseproof paper, and sprinkle half of the hazelnuts on it.
3. Whisk the egg whites with a pinch of the sugar in an electric mixer until you get stiff peaks. Then gradually add the sugar while continuing to mix.
4. Add the rest of the chopped hazelnuts and the vanilla paste. Spread the mixture into the Swiss-roll tin, place straight into the hot oven and bake for 8 minutes. Reduce the heat to 170°C/325°F/Gas Mark 3 and bake for a further 15 minutes.
5. Remove from the oven and turn, hazelnut-side down, onto a sheet of greaseproof paper and allow to cool for 10 minutes. Roll the meringue, from the long side up, as you would a Swiss roll, keeping it tightly rolled.
6. For the toffee sauce, add the sugar and a tablespoon of water to a saucepan. Heat until a slight caramel is formed – about 5 minutes. Then add the butter followed by the cream and golden syrup. Whisk until smooth, then sieve. Allow to cool.
7. Whip the cream until stiff, then add the vanilla paste. Unroll the roulade again and spread some toffee sauce on it, followed by most of the whipped cream. Roll back into shape.
8. Dust with icing sugar and decorate with the remaining whipped cream, a drizzle of toffee sauce and the mint leaves.

Apple and Blackberry Pudding

This pudding is a great supper-time snack or dessert. You can try different combinations with this recipe by including other fruits or adding chocolate chips.

SERVES 12

275 g granulated sugar

275 g butter, softened

2 large cooking apples, peeled and
   thinly sliced

2 large eggs

Drop of vanilla essence

50 ml milk

450 g self-raising flour, sieved

12 blackberries

BRIAN'S TIP

Replace the blackberries with
blueberries or strawberries.

1. Add 50 g sugar and 50 g butter to the sliced apples, and then cook gently in a small pot to soften – about 6 minutes. Leave aside to cool.

2. Preheat the oven to 170°C/325°F/Gas Mark 3.

3. In a bowl, beat the remaining 225 g butter with an electric mixer until light and creamy. Add the remaining 225 g sugar and continue to beat.

4. Beat the eggs separately, and then add with the vanilla essence to the mixture. Keep beating until the mixture is light.

5. Beat in the milk and then add the sieved flour. Gently fold the flour in with a spatula, not the electric mixer.

6. Spoon the cooled apples and the blackberries into the mixture and fold gently through – don't incorporate completely – for a marbled effect. Grease 12 individual moulds or ramekins with butter and fill.

7. Bake for 30 minutes. Serve warm with lashings of custard or ice-cream.

BRIAN'S TIP

Replace the pears with figs
or apricots for a sweeter and
fruitier flavour.

Pear and Almond Tart

This is one of my all-time favourite desserts and it's also my mother's favourite. If you've ever gone to a cake sale, you'll notice the pear and almond tart always sells first, so if you want to make money for a local charity, then this is the one to bring along.

MAKES ONE 25 CM TART

For the pastry

500 g plain flour

125 g sugar

250 g butter, softened

1 egg

For the frangipane

150 g butter, softened

150 g caster sugar

2 eggs

150 g plain flour

150 g ground almonds

A few drops of quality
   almond extract

For the filling

50 g raspberry jam

1 tin of pears, drained

60 g flaked almonds

Whipped cream, for serving

1. Preheat the oven to 200°C/400°F/Gas Mark 6. Grease a 25 cm flan tin.

2. For the pastry, sieve the flour into a bowl. Add the sugar and mix together. Rub in the softened butter until it becomes a sandy texture. Add the egg and combine to form the pastry. Knead and shape in a ball then chill for 20 minutes.

3. Once chilled, roll the pastry out on a floured surface and use it to line the greased flan tin. Trim off any excess.

4. Place a disc of greaseproof paper on the pastry and fill with blind baking beans. Bake for 15 minutes, then remove the baking beans and paper. Return the pastry case to the oven for a further 5 minutes, then remove and allow to cool.

5. For the frangipane, cream the butter and sugar together in a mixer. Mix in the eggs, sieved flour and ground almonds. Add the almond extract and stir.

6. To assemble, spread the raspberry jam on the pastry and add half the frangipane filling, spreading it gently out to the edges. Drain the pears, cut each into 3 wedges and arrange on top of the filling. Dot the remaining frangipane around the pears. Don't worry about spreading this layer out, as it will find its way to the sides when it bakes. Sprinkle with flaked almonds and bake for 30 minutes. Allow to cool in the tin.

7. Serve with whipped cream.

WHAT'S FOR DINNER, DADDY?

Even if I've been out cooking all day, when I get home there's still the dinner to be made! Our daughters, Niamh and Aoife, have always been interested in the food they eat and where it comes from – especially when it comes to helping me taste new recipes at home. I think they must have been to just about every food festival in Ireland, and these days they're brilliant assistants when I'm doing food demonstrations. Now they're fifteen and thirteen, but they're still the most important people I cook for. After all, we all want to give our kids the best start in life, and at that age food is fuel to help them grow and develop. My brothers and I are all six-foot-four, so clearly our mum put some magic in our food! These recipes are all healthy and easy to make and are among Niamh and Aoife's top ten dinners.

Make Us a Burger, Daddy

Burgers – and I mean good homemade burgers – have made a great comeback recently, and rightly so. They are nutritious and amazing to eat when you know what you are putting in them. Any good burger is about quality meat and, for me, a fried, diced onion inside the burger is key. So, when our daughters ask me for a burger, it's the real deal they're after.

SERVES 4

For the burgers

1 small onion, diced

Rapeseed oil, for frying

40 g butter

400 g quality minced beef

1 egg

30 g breadcrumbs

Pinch of nutmeg

50 g Cheddar cheese, grated

To serve

4 brioche burger buns

Burger relish or ploughman's pickle
  (see page 28)

1 beef tomato, sliced

Gem lettuce

BRIAN'S TIP

Try with turkey or pork mince for a different flavoured burger.

1. Preheat the oven to 170°C/325°F/Gas Mark 3.

2. Fry the diced onion in the oil and butter.

3. Place the minced beef in a bowl, then add the cooked onion, egg, breadcrumbs and nutmeg. Add the grated cheese, combine and form 4 equal-sized burgers. Chill in the fridge for 15 minutes.

4. Heat a pan and fry the burgers for 2 minutes on each side. Transfer to a baking tray and place in the oven for 6 minutes. Use the pan the burgers were cooked in to toast the split buns and soak up any juices.

5. Dress the burgers with some relish or pickle, a slice of beef tomato and some gem lettuce. Remember the cheese is melting inside the burger meat.

Aoife's Breaded Chicken Goujons

Ever since Aoife was small, she's claimed her homemade chicken goujons are the best ever – and, you know what, I think she's right. Here is Aoife's best ever chicken goujon recipe.

SERVES 4

---

50 g breadcrumbs

Freshly ground black pepper

4 chicken breasts

50 g plain flour

3 eggs, beaten

50 ml rapeseed oil

25 g butter

AOIFE'S TIP

For a nutty and crispy crumb, try adding some sesame seeds to the breadcrumbs.

1. Preheat the oven to 190°C/375°F/Gas Mark 5.
2. Season the breadcrumbs with pepper.
3. Cut each chicken breast into 5 strips. Dip each chicken piece in the plain flour, then in the beaten egg and, finally, coat in the breadcrumbs.
4. Heat a pan and add a drizzle of oil and the butter. Fry the goujons on both sides until golden brown. Place them on a tray and transfer to the oven for 8 minutes to finish cooking.
5. Remove from the oven and serve with Granny's Homemade Chips (see page 160).

Granny's Homemade Chips

Many's an argument's been had over how to make the perfect chip. No matter how I make them in our house, I'm always told they're not as good as Granny's. I've finally accepted this and, secretly, I agree that my mother's chips really are the best. She peels and cuts the potatoes by hand, which is the key to a good chip.

SERVES 4

---

1 kg potatoes (preferably Roosters)

1 litre cooking oil

1. Peel and cut the potatoes by hand into thick, natural chips.
2. Heat the oil in a deep fat fryer to 130°C/270°F and blanch about ⅓ of the chips for 8 minutes without colouring. Remove and set aside, then repeat until all the chips are blanched.
3. Turn the temperature of the fryer up to 190°C/375°F and cook about ⅓ of the blanched chips for 4–5 minutes until golden and cooked. Repeat until all the chips are done.
4. Serve immediately.

BRIAN'S TIP

Always follow your mother's advice!

Mammy's Leftover Dinner

Brenda makes a great bolognese but she always makes so much that we have it for about three days afterwards. We now call day three Mammy's Leftover Dinner, as that's when she adds chilli to the recipe – sometimes a lot of chilli!

SERVES 4 FOR 3 DAYS

Drizzle of rapeseed oil

1 kg minced beef

4 onions, chopped

6 cloves of garlic, sliced

4 carrots, chopped

3 bay leaves

1 glass red wine

1 tbsp dried oregano

4 tins chopped tomatoes

100 g tomato puree

2 litres beef stock

Handful of fresh basil, chopped

Brenda's leftover ingredient

1 tsp dried chilli flakes

1. In a large pot, heat the oil and brown the minced beef. Then add the onions, garlic and carrots. Add the bay leaves and cook for 5 minutes.

2. Add the red wine and oregano and simmer for 2–3 minutes. Then add the chopped tomatoes and tomato puree with the beef stock.

3. Bring to the boil and allow to simmer for an hour, stirring frequently. The sauce should have a slightly thick consistency. Serve with pasta and some chopped basil sprinkled on top.

4. On day three, add the chilli to the remaining sauce and serve with rice.

BRENDA'S TIP

If you don't want to eat it three days in a row, freeze it in portions – you can use takeaway containers with lids.

Niamh's Favourite Lasagne

I believe every child or young adult should know how to make some version of lasagne. Niamh includes carrots in her lasagne. The reason? She likes them. I taught Niamh this recipe years ago, and now she's made it her own. She's even appeared with me on RTÉ's *Today Show* recently, so watch this space, she tells me!

SERVES 6

For the meat sauce

Drizzle of rapeseed oil

500 g minced beef

1 onion, finely chopped

4 cloves of garlic, crushed

1 carrot, chopped

2 tsp dried oregano

Glass of red wine

75 g tomato puree

400 g tinned chopped tomatoes

Freshly ground black pepper

350 ml beef stock

For the white sauce

70 g butter

70 g plain flour

700 ml milk

1 bay leaf

Pinch of nutmeg

Freshly ground black pepper

100 g Cheddar cheese

For the lasagne

300 g lasagne sheets

30 g Parmesan cheese

1. Preheat the oven to 200°C/400°F/Gas Mark 6.
2. Heat a pot, add a drizzle of oil and brown the meat. Add the chopped onion, garlic and carrot and cook for 4–5 minutes. Add the oregano.
3. Add the wine and allow it to reduce by half. Then add the tomato puree and chopped tomatoes. Season with freshly ground black pepper. Add the beef stock and allow to simmer for 1 hour, stirring occasionally.
4. While the meat is simmering, make the white sauce by melting the butter in a saucepan and adding the flour. Cook for 2 minutes, then add the milk, bay leaf, nutmeg and pepper and allow the sauce to thicken, whisking all the time. Once thickened, add half the grated Cheddar and then put the sauce aside.
5. Soak the lasagne sheets in warm water for at least 15 minutes before assembling.
6. Spoon a thin layer of meat sauce into an ovenproof dish, then a little cheese sauce. Put a layer of lasagne on top. Repeat.
7. Sprinkle the final layer of lasagne sheets and cheese sauce with the remaining Cheddar and the Parmesan.
8. Bake for 1 hour. Allow to stand for 10 minutes before serving.

NIAMH'S TIP

Get your daddy to do the washing up.

Lazy Saturday Omelette

There's nothing like a lazy Saturday morning, but what do you do when it's nearly lunchtime and you've missed breakfast? Omelettes are the easy answer, and when made properly they taste amazing and can work with almost any ingredients. I've chosen bacon, tomatoes and basil for this recipe, but omelettes are so versatile that you can experiment with virtually anything.

SERVES 1

2 slices dry-cured bacon

3 eggs

Freshly ground black pepper

Knob of butter

1 tomato, diced

30 g Cheddar cheese, grated

Handful of fresh basil

BRIAN'S TIP

If you have a few people to feed, treble the recipe and make it in a larger pan. Slice your omelette like a breakfast pizza.

1. Warm your grill to a medium heat.
2. Place the bacon slices on a tray and grill for 5 minutes, turning halfway through.
3. Crack the eggs into a bowl and season with pepper. Using a fork, whisk the eggs until they're light and bubbly.
4. Heat a non-stick omelette pan over a medium heat and melt a knob of butter. Add the beaten eggs to the pan and stir using a spatula, then allow the eggs to settle in the pan and cook for 1 minute.
5. Add the chopped tomatoes and cooked bacon slices on top of the omelette and sprinkle the cheese over. Place the pan under the grill for 2 minutes. The omelette will puff up slightly.
6. Loosen it from the pan and fold it over onto itself. Serve with fresh basil scattered on top.

Hearty Chicken Dinner

Chicken thighs taste amazing yet they are often overlooked. This recipe is as easy a chicken dinner as you'll ever make, and one that everyone in our house loves. It's a sure-fire winner when we're having the 'What's for dinner, Daddy?' conversation.

SERVES 6

Freshly ground black pepper

50 g plain flour

8 chicken thighs

Drizzle of rapeseed oil

1 bay leaf

3 cloves of garlic, crushed

1 small onion, diced

1 carrot, peeled and diced

Half a leek, sliced

5 mushrooms, sliced

Splash of white wine

500 ml chicken stock, warmed

75 ml cream

Fresh parsley, chopped

1. Add a few twists of black pepper to the flour, then coat the chicken thighs.
2. Heat a casserole dish, add a drizzle of rapeseed oil and lightly fry the chicken until golden.
3. Add a bay leaf and the garlic followed by the onion, carrot, leek and mushrooms, stirring in between adding each vegetable.
4. Add a splash of wine and let it simmer for 5 minutes. Then add the warm chicken stock. Pop on a lid and simmer for 15 minutes. Then remove the lid, stir and add the cream. Simmer for a further 45 minutes with the lid on.
5. Remove from the heat and garnish with chopped parsley.

BRIAN'S TIP

Sweet potato or butternut squash is also great in this dish. Serve with boiled rice or mashed potato and cabbage.

Chicken Fried Rice – With No Peas, Daddy!

'Can we have chicken fried rice but with no peas?' It's a lazy Sunday-evening dish often demanded in our house. I actually love it with peas and add them in after I've made it for the girls. It's easy to make and way more healthy than a takeaway version.

SERVES 4

Drizzle of rapeseed oil

200 g chicken breast, diced

1 knob of fresh ginger, grated

4 cloves of garlic, chopped

600 g long grain rice, cooked

4 scallions, chopped

Freshly ground black pepper

4 eggs

Optional

100 g frozen peas, added with the rice

1. In a wok, heat the oil and add the chicken. Cook for 4 minutes, stirring all the time.
2. Add the ginger and garlic, cook for a further 3 minutes then add the cooked rice.
3. Allow the rice to heat through. Then add the chopped scallions and season with pepper.
4. Beat the eggs together in a bowl and add to the wok, stirring them in quickly. This will give you fluffy cooked-egg strands throughout the rice.

BRIAN'S TIP

Replace the chicken with ham or bacon. Sprinkle with toasted sesame seeds.

Easy Meatballs

Please, please, don't buy pre-made meatballs – honestly, they only take minutes to make at home and it can be lots of fun if you involve everyone in the process. And don't even think about buying ready-made sauce either! This recipe has everything you need to make your own incredible meatballs.

SERVES 4

For the sauce

Drizzle of rapeseed oil

1 onion, diced

2 cloves of garlic, chopped

1 tsp dried oregano

400 g tinned, chopped tomatoes

50 g tomato puree

500 ml beef stock

For the meatballs

Drizzle of rapeseed oil

1 onion, diced

1 clove of garlic, chopped

250 g minced beef

250 g minced pork

1 egg

40 g breadcrumbs

½ tsp ground nutmeg

Freshly ground black pepper

5 fresh sage leaves, chopped

To serve

400 g spaghetti

80 g Parmesan cheese, for grating

1. To make the sauce, heat a drizzle of oil in a saucepan and sweat the onion with the garlic for 3 minutes. Add the oregano, tomatoes and tomato puree. Add the stock and simmer for 10 minutes, stirring occasionally.

2. For the meatballs, fry the diced onion and garlic in the oil in a heated frying pan. Add these to a bowl with the minced beef and pork. Combine using your hands and then add the egg and breadcrumbs and season with nutmeg and pepper. Mix well, then add the chopped sage leaves and shape into desired meatball size.

3. In the same frying pan you cooked the onions in, brown the meatballs then transfer them into the sauce. Simmer together for 12 minutes, stirring gently to ensure the meatballs don't break.

4. Cook the spaghetti in boiling water according to the packet instructions and then drain. Serve in a bowl with meatballs and sauce on top and some grated Parmesan cheese.

BRIAN'S TIP

The meatball recipe makes tasty, succulent burger meat—just shape into burgers instead of meatballs.

Lamb Steak Sandwich with Mint Yoghurt

When we think of a steak sandwich we automatically think of beef, but it's a great light sandwich when made with lamb. Your butcher will give you lamb steaks for this recipe and I've often made lots of little mini lamb-steak sandwiches as canapes using this recipe.

SERVES 4

4 lamb steaks

50 ml rapeseed oil

2 cloves of garlic, sliced

Zest of 1 lemon

Bunch of fresh mint leaves, chopped

4 slices ciabatta bread

1 beef tomato, sliced into 4

Handful of rocket leaves

To serve

50 g natural yoghurt

4 fresh mint leaves, chopped

Freshly ground black pepper

50 g tomato chutney

1. Put the lamb steaks on a plate and allow to come to room temperature. Then add a drizzle of rapeseed oil, the garlic, lemon zest and mint leaves.

2. Heat a frying pan and add the steaks. Cook on each side for about 2 minutes.

3. While the steaks are cooking, toast the ciabatta bread. Place a slice of tomato and some rocket leaves on each piece of bread.

4. Leave the lamb to rest for a few minutes and then slice. Arrange it on top of the rocket leaves.

5. Add the 4 chopped mint leaves to the yoghurt and put a dollop on top of each lamb steak.

6. Season with black pepper and serve with tomato chutney.

BRIAN'S TIP

Try serving with potato wedges (see page 113) or boiled baby new potatoes with rosemary.

COOKING AND CRAIC

One of the best parts of a Donegal get-together is the craic, so if you're doing the cooking you want to make sure you don't miss anything! Some of the best food I've eaten has been in the company of friends, and I've always believed that food is a key part of any successful gathering. What's best of all, of course, is food that can be shared, so when we're having people over I like to go for big dishes that allow everyone to get stuck in and help themselves. These are my top recipes for tear-and-share food – and for getting the craic flowing!

Herby Roast Leg of Donegal Lamb

Donegal has the most sheep of any county in Ireland. Believe it or not, there are a staggering 495,163 sheep in Donegal (and that's not just me saying it – it's from the sheep census as reported by the *Farmer's Journal*). So we know how to rear them! I honestly believe we have the best lamb in Ireland here in Donegal.

SERVES 6–8

4 cloves of garlic, peeled

5 sprigs of thyme

6 mint leaves

2 sprigs of rosemary

Freshly ground black pepper

Drizzle of rapeseed oil

Zest of 1 lemon

1 leg of lamb (roughly 2kg)

2 potatoes, peeled and cut into quarters

2 onions, halved

2 carrots, peeled and halved

Splash of red wine

100 ml hot chicken stock

1 tbsp tomato puree

BRIAN'S TIP

Slice leftover lamb and use it to fill some naan breads with a little mint yoghurt dip (see page 171) for an evening snack.

1. Preheat the oven to 170°C/325°F/Gas Mark 3.
2. Using a pestle and mortar, crush the peeled garlic with the thyme, mint, rosemary and black pepper. Add a drizzle of oil and the lemon zest.
3. Rub the mixture over the whole surface of the lamb.
4. Place the potatoes, onions and carrots in a roasting dish and rest the lamb on top of the vegetables.
5. Cover the lamb with tin foil. Roast in the oven for two hours, or until cooked to your liking.
6. When cooked, remove the lamb and set on a tray to rest for at least 15 minutes before carving.
7. While the meat is resting, place the roasting dish on the hob over a medium heat and add a splash of red wine and then the hot stock. Stir with a wooden spoon, scraping up anything that's stuck to the tray, and mash the vegetables to thicken the gravy.
8. Add 250 ml of boiling water and the tomato puree and allow to simmer for 10 minutes. Strain and pour your gravy over the freshly carved lamb.

Inishowen Whiskey-Glazed Chicken Wings

I can't think of an occasion when great tasting chicken wings don't steal the show. I'm using Inishowen Irish Whiskey to enhance this recipe, as it has a perfect balance of malt and grain with a hint of peat. It's produced by Cooley Distillery, and the bottle features a picture of Burt Castle, which you can see from the window of my parents' house.

SERVES 4

For the barbecue sauce

Drizzle of rapeseed oil

1 onion, finely diced

4 cloves of garlic, crushed

100 g brown sugar

80 ml apple cider vinegar

40 g tomato puree

300 g tomato ketchup

Few shakes of Worcestershire sauce

100 ml Inishowen Irish Whiskey

For the chicken

1 kg chicken wings

Freshly ground black pepper

5 sprigs of thyme

1 lime, cut into wedges

1. Preheat the oven to 190°C/375°F/Gas Mark 5.
2. To make the barbecue sauce, heat the rapeseed oil, add the onion and sweat. Add the garlic and then the sugar and cook for 2 minutes. Then add the vinegar, tomato puree and tomato ketchup and allow the sauce to simmer for 8 minutes. Add the Worcestershire sauce and whiskey and simmer for a further 5 minutes.
3. Season the chicken wings with pepper and thyme, then place on a tray in the oven and cook for 35 minutes.
4. Remove and drizzle the sauce over the wings. Then return to the oven for a further 15 minutes until sticky.
5. Serve with the wedges of fresh lime.

BRIAN'S TIP

Keep a bit of extra sauce for dipping. The sauce will keep in the fridge for 4 weeks and is perfect for a barbecue.

Porky Pies All Round

Everyone tells porky pies occasionally but there's no lying about the superb taste of these hand-held snacks. They speak for themselves and are a great finger food for an evening gathering. Once you have mastered the pastry, you can include other ingredients in the filling such as leeks, smoked bacon or cheese.

MAKES 12

For the pastry

125 ml water

110 g butter

350 g plain flour

1 egg yolk

1 egg, beaten, to glaze

For the filling

450 g minced pork

1 apple, peeled and grated

60 ml water

1 tsp dried sage

½ tsp dried thyme

½ tsp dried parsley

Freshly ground black pepper

BRIAN'S TIP

Bake these pies in advance, freeze them and then reheat for a party (25 minutes at 170°C/325°F/Gas Mark 3).

1. Preheat the oven to 180°C/350°F/Gas Mark 4. Grease a 12-cup muffin tin.
2. To make the pastry, heat the water and butter in a saucepan. Boil for 2 minutes.
3. Remove from the heat and add the flour and egg yolk and combine well by stirring briskly for a few minutes. Allow to cool and then knead on a floured surface for 4–5 minutes. Cover the dough and leave at room temperature for 30 minutes.
4. While the dough is resting, make the filling by simply mixing all the ingredients together.
5. Roll out the pastry fairly thinly (about 5 mm) on a floured surface and cut into discs twice the size of the individual muffin cups in the tin.
6. Line each cup of the tin with a pastry disc. Fill each one with the pie filling. Roll out the remaining pastry and cut out smaller discs for the pie lids. Brush some beaten egg around the edges of the pastry cases and pop the lids on top. Press down around the edges to seal. Then glaze the top of each pie with some more beaten egg.
7. Cook in the centre of the oven for about 45 minutes or until golden.

Braised Beef Cheeks

Braised beef cheeks are very popular on restaurant menus these days, and they go down really well too when made for family or friends. Plus, if you're doing the cooking, it's a stress-free one-pot dish, which gives you more time to socialise with your guests.

SERVES 4

Drizzle of rapeseed oil

4 beef cheeks from your butcher (you may need to request them in advance)

1 onion, finely chopped

1 carrot, peeled and finely chopped

2 sticks of celery, diced

1 bay leaf

Freshly ground black pepper

400 ml red wine

400 g chopped tomatoes

1. Preheat the oven to 160°C/325°F/Gas Mark 3.
2. Heat the rapeseed oil in an ovenproof pot. Brown the beef cheeks on all sides, and then add the onion, carrot, celery and bay leaf. Cook for 10 minutes, agitating the vegetables occasionally, and season with pepper.
3. Add the wine and tomatoes and simmer for 15 minutes. Then place a tight-fitting lid on top and cook for 3 hours in the oven.
4. The cheeks will fall apart when cooked.
5. Serve with large pasta shapes or poundies (see page 106).

BRIAN'S TIP

Beef cheeks are so tasty when cooked this way. You can even use the beef in between layers of lasagne (see page 162).

Rack of Ribs to Die For

Get these ribs into the centre of a table and you will be adored by all, I promise! The only way to enjoy these ribs is to tear and share – get stuck in there, eat with your hands and lick the sauce off your fingers. This type of food is ideal for social eating and really gets the conversation going.

SERVES 4

For the marinade

½ fresh red chilli, finely chopped

3 cloves of garlic, chopped

75 ml apple juice

100 ml white wine vinegar

60 ml soy sauce

50 g soft brown sugar

50 g honey

3 tsp tomato ketchup

1 tsp Dijon mustard

1 thumb-sized piece of ginger

For the ribs

1 rack of ribs (about 1 kg)

Drizzle of rapeseed oil

Freshly ground black pepper

2 sprigs of rosemary

10 basil leaves, chopped

1 lime, cut into wedges

1. Preheat the oven to 200°C/400°F/Gas Mark 6.
2. For the marinade, place all the ingredients in a pot and mix. Bring to the boil, and then reduce the heat and simmer for about 15 mins, stirring occasionally. The sauce will thicken.
3. Place the ribs in a large roasting dish. Drizzle with rapeseed oil, season with black pepper and sprinkle with the fresh rosemary. Spread the marinade over the ribs and place a lid on the roasting dish. Roast in the oven for 1 hour, then baste the ribs with the sauce from the dish and cook for a further 20 minutes.
4. The ribs will be ready to eat, but if you wish you can transfer to a barbecue for a few minutes for extra flavour.
5. Serve with chopped basil leaves and lime wedges.

BRIAN'S TIP

Don't forget to serve with a bowl of warm water and a lemon slice to help clean sticky hands!

Black Pudding Dipping Fritters

Black pudding is a nutritional 'superfood' according to many sources, but I was already a fan based purely on its flavour, and I'm lucky to have some of the best black pudding in the country available locally. Using pudding to create these tasty dippers is a little different and makes a great starter.

SERVES 12

For the filling

300 g black pudding

1 apple, peeled and grated

40 g butter

6 leaves of fresh sage

For the crumb

200 g breadcrumbs

100 g porridge oats

50 g flour

3 eggs, beaten

1 litre vegetable oil, for frying

Apple chutney, to serve

1. Preheat the oven to 170°C/325°F/Gas Mark 3.

2. To make the black pudding filling, simply place all the ingredients in a blender and blend until combined. Then shape into round, bite-size shapes.

3. Next, mix the breadcrumbs and porridge oats together. Roll each dipper in the flour and then the beaten egg. Then finely coat them in the breadcrumb and porridge-oat mix.

4. Heat the oil in a deep fat fryer or deep pot to 170°C/325°F. Fry the puddings until golden in colour. Place on a tray and cook in the oven for 5 minutes.

5. Serve with some apple chutney for dipping.

BRIAN'S TIP

Try with white pudding or minced raw pork instead of black pudding.

Hand-Held Baby Quiche

Eggs are easily the most versatile ingredient to have in your kitchen, and when it comes to having friends over, this is the tastiest snack food you can prepare in minutes. Brenda's dad, Seamus, keeps hens and we are very lucky to have fresh eggs every day. If you can get just-laid eggs, it will give your baby quiche a richer colour and taste.

MAKES 12

---

12 sheets of filo pastry

3 eggs

4 rashers of bacon, diced

6 scallions , finely chopped

50 g Cheddar cheese, grated

50 ml cream

Freshly ground black pepper

Handful of fresh chives, chopped

1. Preheat the oven to 180°C/350°F/Gas Mark 4. Lightly grease a 12-cup muffin tin.
2. Using one sheet per cup, quickly fold the filo pastry in half and then in half again and push down into the base and sides of each muffin cup. Repeat until all 12 are lined.
3. In a bowl, mix the eggs, bacon, scallions, cheese, cream, pepper and chives.
4. Divide the egg mix between the muffin tins. Bake in the oven for 15–20 minutes or until golden brown. Remove to a wire rack to cool.

BRIAN'S TIP

Replace the bacon with ham and serve with a dollop of crème fraiche on top.

Goat's Cheese Tartlets

Goat's cheese is sweet and when heated with red onion chutney it tastes mild and delicious. I've suggested making these as individual tartlets, but this recipe will work just as well as a large 25 cm tart.

MAKES 12

4 red onions, thinly sliced

Drizzle of rapeseed oil

150 g dark brown sugar

60 ml balsamic vinegar

60 ml red wine

1 packet puff pastry

150 g good quality roasted red peppers from a jar, sliced

120 g soft goat's cheese

120 ml cream

Few sprigs of thyme

1. Preheat the oven to 190°C/375°F/Gas Mark 5. Grease a 12-cup muffin tray.
2. Fry the red onions in a drizzle of oil for 4–5 minutes. Then add the sugar to caramelise them. Cook on a low heat for a further 5 minutes until slightly sticky.
3. Add the balsamic vinegar and red wine and allow to simmer for 15 minutes.
4. Roll out 400 g of the puff pastry. Cut out 12 large discs with a biscuit cutter and use them to line each greased cup of the muffin tin.
5. Place a piece of roasted red pepper in the base of each cup with some of the onion mix. Add the goat's cheese on top. Pour in a dollop of cream and top with a sprig of fresh thyme leaves.
6. Place in the oven and bake for 30 minutes or until the pastry is golden.

BRIAN'S TIP

Add some pesto on top of the cheese for an even tastier version.

Index